BUCKSKIN BESSIE

HER LOST LETTERS

BUCKSKIN BESSIE

HER LOST LETTERS

Monica James

Buckskin Press
7704 W. John Cabot Rd.
Glendale, Arizona 85308
Websites: www.BuckskinPress.com
           www.Buckskinbessie@cox.net

Library of Congress Cataloging-in-Publication Data

James, Monica.
   Buckskin Bessie : her lost letters / [Monica James]. -- [1st ed.]

      p. : ill. ; cm.
   Includes bibliographical references.

1. Buckskin Bessie. 2. Miller Bros. & Arlington 101 Ranch Real Wild West (Show)--People.   3. Cowgirls--Oklahoma--Biography.   4. Women entertainers--Oklahoma--Biography. 5. Wild west shows. 6. West (U.S.)--Biography. I. Title.

GV1833 .J36 2005
791.84/092

ISBN: 0-9773711-051495

Printed in the United States of America
Library of Congress Control Number: 2005910281

Book Consultant: Five Star Publications, Inc.
                    Linda F. Radke, President
                    P.O. Box 6698, Chandler, Arizona 85246-6698
                    480-940-8182

Cover Design: Brian Higgins

Disclaimer: These typed letters are the representation of the original letters written and no offense is intended for any single person or group of persons. The information included in this book is either documented or is of the author's opinion for the purpose of inspiring further thought on the subject. Every effort has been made to be accurate and give all other sources credit and due recognition.

Dedicated to Bettie Amanda Herberg Carter Blackwell

"Buckskin Bessie"

Gone but not forgotten.

"The best book is collaboration between author and reader"

Barbara Tuchman, Historian

Contents

Acknowledgments

A special note of gratitude to the following people:

Betty Hislop Fillion, wherever you are, for valuing relationship enough to save these letters.

Wess James, my stepson who rescued them.

Bessie's family members, who generously gave me their support and shared their many pictures and stories.

My husband, Bob, who walks by my side.

Judy Roberts, who prodded and inspired me from the very beginning and offered invaluable advice.

All the previous authors and historians who paved the road.

And most of all, the Lord, the creator of all.

Foreword

Today we celebrate the Old West in both reality and legend. Rodeo is one of America's most popular sports, evolving from early-day competitions between ranches before going on to become a national institution. Performers and aficionados reenact historical events featuring the lives of frontier soldiers, fur trappers and settlers. Tourists come to the American West from all over the world to visit real frontier towns like Tombstone, Arizona, to witness shoot-outs such as the reenactment of the famous "Gunfight at OK Corral," or mythical towns, ones with false-front buildings as can be seen at Rawhide in Scottsdale.

Even while the Old West was still alive, real-life adventurers like Buffalo Bill Cody, Pawnee Bell (Gordon Lillie), and Texas Jack Omohundro thrilled audiences with trick riding, sharpshooting, daring simulated attacks by real Indians on stagecoaches, along with such cowboy contests as riding, roping, and steer wrestling. At first, it was a purely local attraction. Before long, the shows were playing before large audiences in England and Europe. After performing for Queen Victoria's Golden Jubilee in 1887, Cody's show returned two years later for a four-year European tour.

Another spectacular Wild West show was the Miller Brother's 101 Ranch at Ponca City, Oklahoma, which featured such well-known western figures as Buck Jones, Bill Pickett, and Geronimo. Superstars Tom Mix and Will Rogers performed in their early years with the 101 outfit.

The heyday for Wild West shows ended in the 1930s, but during their time they glamorized for much of the world the last frontier, introducing the cowboy hero and opening the way for western novels, movies, and television shows.

I've just presented a brief historical overview of the Wild West show to set the stage for Monica James' wonderful insight into one of those performers. As she mentions in her prologue, "History should be more than just a documentation of dates and events; it should include the experiences and personalities of those who lived it." History tells us how it was, but literature tells us how it felt.

I gave you a little of the history and dates, and now Monica is going to take you beyond the façade of that beautiful lady feathered on the Wild West poster and introduce you to the real Bessie Herberg Carter Blackwell.

Marshall Trimble
Arizona's Official State Historian
2004

Prologue

he surfacing of a mysterious packet of old letters was the fuel that propelled the writing of this book. Letters that had been carelessly tossed onto a pile of rubble at an estate sale with only the bright red letters "101 Wild West Show" peeking out. Research revealed that although unknown to some, the 101 Wild West Show was just as famous as those staged by Buffalo Bill and Pawnee Bill and equaled their success. The opportunity to retrieve the two old photo albums that had also been left behind gave credence to the names written in the letters and faces loomed up and matched. Deeper research produced remaining family members with stories of their own to tell and earlier publications documented and paralleled the matching history.

Buckskin Bessie, who was also known as Montana Bess, was not as famous as such performers of the 101 Wild West Show as Lucille Mulhall, Will Rogers, Ruth Roach, and Bill Picket to name a few. Nonetheless, she was far more than just another performer. She was also the documented lover/companion of the owner of the Wild West show, Joe Miller, and their relationship lasted longer than many marriages, close to 15 years.

Bessie has been categorized, as have so many others who have lived before us (a fault that has been part of our civilization for centuries). Some would have you believe that she was a cheap, kept woman, with no other means for success in life. Others may lead you to believe that she was an extraordinarily gifted and daring individual who was destined to live a life of luxury and fame. Still others portray her as a young beauty who was taken advantage of and led astray. Bessie's handwritten letters give us, the readers, the opportunity to see her as she really was: an individual who, like us, had strengths and weaknesses, talents and opportunities, and with them made the decisions that formed her life.

These letters are sketchy at times and do not give us all the information we would like, but I invite you join me in the search of who was really the victim and who was the villain and ponder why it all ended in tragedy.

History should be more than just a documentation of dates and events; it should include the experiences and personalities of those who lived it. Rarely are we afforded the privilege, as these letters provide, to step back in time, to visit an era with a different set of rules and expectations, where simplicity was the norm and Wild West shows the exception.

Introduction

James Collection

he beautiful young woman seated on the right wrote the following letters to her older sister, Esther Herberg Boomh Patwell (on the left). They provide the solid information for this biography rather than the faint memories of some or the eager promotion of others.

Letter writing has become a lost art but in the 1800s and early 1900s students were taught penmanship and they labored long hours to improve their writing skills. With the invention of the telephone, people were no longer dependent on letter writing to correspond and consequently we lost the documentation of people's thoughts and feelings. Documentation, that while reading it, brings them back to life with each stroke of the pen.

We are first introduced to Bessie as a very young woman who is coming to a crossroad in her life, one that will dictate her entire future. Unlike most of the young women of her day, she had a desire for much more than just marriage and children; she wanted an education and land of her own. How those desires led her down the path of joining a Wild West Show is not clear but join the show, she did.

Becoming a performer in a Wild West show was a not a claim to fame. "Those" women had reputations of being hard, loose in their morals, rebellious to tradition and without proper education; a second-class citizen, if you will. Some performers even wore masks to protect their families from the harsh criticisms that were sure to come.[1]

Amazingly Bessie rarely complains in her letters written home even though life in a Wild West Show was grueling, to say the least. The unbelievable schedules, the monotony of the routines, the harsh weather conditions they often endured and living out of a trunk. Being encamped with groups of people from all walks of life, privacy being nonexistent and the never-ending competition of needing to be young, beautiful and talented could make the difference in your wages and privileges. And last but not least, there was the ever-present danger of injury around every bend. Few performers lasted more than a couple of years.

All of her letters, the copies of the unique letterheads and envelopes are here; they have not been altered or changed. Information has been included from research, references to other publications are stipulated and an array of pictures has been added, but her letters will speak for themselves.

---

[1] *Life in a Wild West Show, pg. 39, Steven Currie*

Chapter 1

Immigrants' Daughter

Bessie's parents, Swedish immigrants
Jonas and Bertha Herberg

Stevens Collection

Buckskin Bessie

Her given name was Bettie Amanda Herberg. Controversy surrounds her, even in the date of her birth. She was the fourth child of seven born to Jonas and Bertha Herberg in Ruthton, Minnesota. A 1900 United States Census form filed by her father states that she was born September 15, 1885 (a fact with which her remaining family members concur). However, on a 1920 United States Census filed by Bettie (Bessie) herself, she states that she was 29 years old in that year, which would mean she'd been born around 1891, a six year discrepancy. Women have tended to lie a little about their age and perhaps this was the situation; but on her headstone, located in Ponca City, Oklahoma, it states her birth as 1896 (that's an 11 year discrepancy). This, as you will learn, turns out to be the most disturbing of all.

There are studies that reveal the personality traits of children according to their birth order (that is, the middle child often having more issues than the other siblings, etc.). Although I cannot validate the accuracy of these studies, according to her family, she was indeed very different from her brothers and sisters. Her remaining family members only knew Bessie when they themselves were children, but these are some of the adjectives they used to describe her: famous, colorful, outspoken, wild, and hyper.

Written on the back:
Bessie on skies in front of the cabin.
James Collection

Immigrants' Daughter

Each individual's handwriting is as unique as their fingerprint and experts in the field can establish identification through the examination and comparison of it. Although it was not feasible to publish the letters in their handwritten form, a sample of her handwriting is of the essence.

The flair found in her penmanship is but a preview to her character and personality. The fact that it slants to the left, her pictures show her with her pin secured on the left side of her blouse, and her hat is curled up on the left side where she grabbed it to give a sweeping bow, leads one to conclude that she most likely was left-handed.

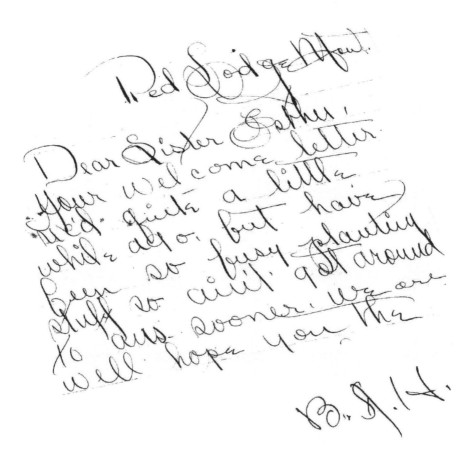

RED LODGE, MONTANA

The county seat of Carbon county, is situated at the foot of the Beartooth mountains and is in the heart of the largest coal belt in the northwest. It has a monthly payroll for this industry alone that exceeds $75,000.

The altitude of the city is 5548 feet. Within an hour's drive is scenery that rivals that of Yellowstone Park. At the present time it has a population of 3500 which is rapidly increasing. It has churches of all denominations and a perfect system of graded schools, also the free county high school.

Rural mail routes and telephone connections reach all parts of the county from this city. Red Lodge has a fine electric light plant and a water works system that furnishes the purest water in the state. The climate is equiable all the year round. The average shipments of coal will exceed 2,500 tons a day.

Red Lodge has the reputation of possessing the finest summer climate in Montana and is the mecca for summer outing parties. The city is substantially constructed. Insurance rates are low, and the town is well protected against fire. The northern part of the county produces annually thousands of tons of sugar beets. Its people are wide-awake and hustling. Carbon county has carried off more prizes at the State Fair than any other county in the state and is noted the state over as the fruit and grain belt of Montana. Red Lodge is situated on the Rocky Fork branch of the Northern Pacific railroad. The city possesses several good hotels and many large stores of all classes. Its banking facilities are ample and are well patronized by the cattle men and ranchers, many of whom make their homes in the city during the winter, thus allowing their childeren the advantages of the excellent city schools.

The first letter in that bundle from the estate sale was in this beautiful envelope. If you read it, you will be amazed at the amount of information given about the little town of Red Lodge, Montana. This was a traveling advertisement! Found tucked between the letter's old yellow pages were dried lilac flowers still intact.

Immigrants' Daughter

June 18, 1907
Red Lodge Mont.

Dear Sister Esther,

Your welcome letter, rec'd quite a little while ago,
but have been so busy planting stuff so ain't got around to
ans. sooner. We are well hope you are the same, we are
having a darn cold spring so guess nothing will grow much.
It must be the same where you are. I shouldn't think
you wouldn't need any more papers if you take so many
and Seth loved my roses are coming along fine. Was
that from your roses inside you sent me? Where do you
get time to read all your papers? Do you go home often,
how does Ma get along now. Does she seem to miss me?
My it must be pretty at home in summer. Arthur told me
there were 30 lilac bushes blossomed last year. Have you
a pretty yard? Don't spose you've had time yet. My I
wish I were going with you to Herman.

I just wrote Alma again but she has not answered.
What do you spose is the reason she does not answer my
letters? Where is Anna Reed now? Should think she
would be getting married.

How does Josie S. look? I wonder how her
and Will get along. How are Carrin and Ole making

Buckskin Bessie

it? Has she got any sense yet? Lily & Maud must be getting to be pretty big girls by this time. What's the matter with you, where's your kids? Or ain't you any good? Maybe it's your old man or maybe you don't want any. I'd want only one.

Do you ever hear from Laura?

So they put Mrs. Axlegrease in jail for 6 months. It ought to been 6 years. Say but she was an old hag if there ever was one.

The last I saw Claire Mouty was when I came through Willmar to N. Dak. He wanted me to go to dinner with him and I did.

So you would come here for a visit. I'm glad of that cause I'll probably have money enough to send your fare. Well it's supper time so guess I'll haf to quit cause I've got 2 cows to milk. After supper I go to bed 8 O'clock. Spose you go to League after supper. Don't wait long as I did. Write quick,

Your Sister,
Beatrice Herberg

Bessie
James Collection

An important fact about this first letter is that she signed her name as, Beatrice Herberg. Upon first reading this, it could appear that this was her given name and Bessie was a nickname, but all of her family refers to her as Bettie and all of the people in Oklahoma called her Bessie. There is only one other document found that referred to her as Beatrice and that was a formal letter from the Forest Department in Montana (a copy of that letter will be seen later); but in truth, her given name was Bettie Amanda Herberg.

Her family was one of thousands who came and homesteaded in the Minnesota area where she was born. Bessie's grandfather and two uncles first emigrated to the U.S. from Sweden in the late 1800s and her father and mother followed in 1878. I gathered the following information from the Pipestone County Atlas 1914: On an Aetna township north, Range 44, West of the 5th P.M. Pipestone County, Minnesota, Jonas Herberg has 8 sections SW 160."

Note: A section is 640 acres. Most homesteaders could only afford to purchase one section.

The first question that arises is "why is Bessie in Red Lodge, Montana, when all her family seems to be established in Minnesota?" Her reference in her letter to "we" implies she is not alone. So who is with her? It was springtime and they were spring planting. This is no small task and usually would require several workers depending on the amount of acreage involved.

Typical of farm workers, her day revolved around the rising and the setting of the sun. She clearly is not afraid of hard work and has learned at a young age to be disciplined, a characteristic that will be required to be part of a traveling Wild West show.

The dried lilac flowers found in this letter of 1907 are but a small representation of Bessie's love of flowers that is apparent throughout her lifetime.

Seth is Esther's husband and Bessie's brother-in-law. Arthur is her younger brother and Alma is her oldest sister. Many other people are mentioned, and it is assumed they were friends and acquaintances, with the exception of Mrs. Axlegrease, of course. Esther and Seth lived in Ruthton, Minnesota. Herman, Minnesota, is located about 135 miles away, and this is possibly where her Ma was. Willmar is also in Minnesota where she says she had dinner with Claire on her way to North Dakota. Now this is in the year of 1907 and she is traveling a lot for a young unmarried woman. This was not only unusual for the traditions of those times, but also in the funds that would have been required to do so.

In the early 1900s most every town of any size had a local newspaper and they were simply called "papers."

Bessie
James Collection

Strange, the questions she asks about her Ma. Was she not corresponding with her herself?

Extra, Extra
Although visitors to Red Lodge today would see little evidence of the bustling activities of the early 1900s the old Northern Pacific Depot is still standing and has been preserved as an historical site.

Without a doubt, Bessie's footprints are part of the heritage found here.

Buckskin Bessie

Oct. 3, 1910
Cedar Falls, Iowa

Dear Sister,

    I commenced school Mon. Have quite a way to go but won't mind it when I get used to it. Can you send the other $5 right away. I had my teeth fixed, hurt so I could not do anything. Had let it run too long. He had to kill the nerve and I thought I'd die before he got through, said it was about the meanest tooth he ever saw.

    Mr. Parsons is going to pay my fare, also tuition. If I am not through in the 5 months I haf to buy 3 books, could not get some second handed. I cannot write more, It is nearly school time.

Bess

Over and over, there will be great gaps of time between the letters that were found in the packet. Only the writer of them, or perhaps the recipient, could tell us why.

The following letter was written three years later and whether or not she has been in Red Lodge, Montana, all that time is not known. Perhaps the biggest question is why would she choose to go all the way to Cedar Falls to attend school? Cedar Falls, Iowa is a very long way from Montana. And who is Mr. Parsons, and why would he pay her fare and tuition?

Immigrants' Daughter

Oct. 12, 1910
Cedar Falls, Iowa

Dear Sister,

I rec'd your letter and will answer today. It is Sunday, has been terrible cold. I believe this is a cold country, it generally is I guess along rivers.

So Daddy wants Seth to come. Spose you are going. Wish it were time for me to go to that country, but will haf to wait quite a while.

I imagine I am getting along fine, but you know it is much slower in High S- than if you were attending Business College, as they cannot devote as much time to you but hope by spring that I will not have much left to learn. I could not very well come home Xmas, it would be foolish, cost more than $10, and I need money too bad to use it foolishly. It seems to take an awful lot of paper and such stuff.

My shoes are about all in and I have no heavy underwear. Wish I had some fleece lined like Ma got that day we were to town.

How does Ma get along with the work?

Did Mother Corey say anything about Kii, you write and ask her all about him.

Buckskin Bessie

I hear from Cosier quite often and Montana. I was to Waterloo. Too bad they lost Frank, he was a mighty good horse.

I never heard anymore from Anntie Reed, after I told her I could not come, it doesn't worry me.

So the Kallestads have left. How's my friend Hermanson, if the old lady did not find it out, you could love him up a little for me.

Tell Emily I will write her if I ever get 5 min. leisure time. I'll tell you, there is not much time for play with yours truly.

Tell Ma that shoes would be a dandy Xmas present for me.

Mr. & Mrs. Parsons have been to Chicago to stock show, were gone a wk. Mazir and I kept house it made us hustle some too, we washed and ironed yesterday, they brought us each a Japanese cup and saucer and me 2 pr. of hose which was a very useful present. The cup and saucer Mrs. Mochl their oldest girl sent us she lives at Cedar Rapids and I have never seen her, The boy Owen is or was in Canada he last crossed over the line and is in Wash. Now. He's only a kid 19 or 20, I have never seen him, but the crazy kid writes to me. He goes all over the country, was intending to take claim

Immigrants' Daughter

in Can. But guess he changed his mind.

Last wk, to hear Billy Sunday, say but he's a peach. He has a tabernacle that covers almost an acre, made of rough lumber and about 300 people sing in the chorus. Has good music. Gee but he gets excited, he runs and jumps and acts as though something were ailing him. Just the same he says a good many sensible things. His text was "Your sins will find you out" I like to hear him would like very much to go again, but we haf to go on streetcars out it is quite late when we get home. I went with the folks, I am saving a lot of his sermons from the Newspaper, if I could write shorthand a little better I might of taken it down.

I do not know if I have ans. your questions or not, you letter is upstairs, don't be so slow in ans.

Your sister,
B. A. H.

"A good gift is a useful one." You cannot be more practical than that, and this trait will be of great importance when she is on the road with the Wild West show and there is room for only the bare necessities. Some Wild West shows were known to only allow one trunk often limited to two feet long and eighteen inches high to hold all of your personal belongings.

Below is a small clip from a web site of Billy Sunday. He was a very famous evangelist about whom much has been written over the years. My understanding is that his recurring theme was "Your sins will find you out." He would burst onto the stage in a dead run and slide up to the pulpit and yell, "Your Sins will find you out!" One of his websites included a schedule of the locations and dates of the revivals he held and sure enough, he was in Cedar Falls at the time of this letter.

Come to think of it, "Your sins will find you out" could very well have been the subtitle of this book, with all the suspicious events that occur and the mysteries that unfold.

Billy Sunday (1862 – 1935)
American Evangelist

Riding the streetcar to the tent revival? Visions of a horse-drawn streetcar come to mind.

Bessie uses the phrase "the folks" a lot, but as you continue to read, it becomes clear she is not referring to her mother and father.

This was probably a term of endearment that was popular at the time. In this letter, she included a sample of her shorthand that she was studying. It is her name, the words "write soon" and the name of Esther's cat.

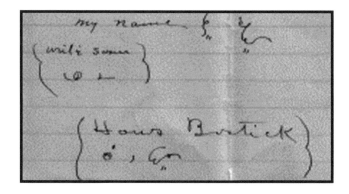

Dear Sister,

Rec. your letter today and will ans. right away while I am drying my hair. Not a very nice day for anyone to wash their hair, regular blizzards, gee I hate this open country. We never have these d- blizzards in the Mts. I had a letter from Daddy yesterday. Just a short one, said he had just returned from somewhere and would write me more when he got home. I expect he wants me to come back, but won't, not without I have a place of my own cause he won't let me have a man I want. I'm going to be my own boss after this.

We have had 2 wks. vacation and I'm nearly bug-house, I never was so lonesome before. I do not know if I will go to school or not. It's not because I do not like to, cause I'm just crazy to learn and nothing I'd rather do than use the 7 winter. But I'll tell you as you can see why I not satisfied with things. I asked

Buckskin Bessie

Miss Dobry, our teacher, how long we would haf to go before we got our diplomas, She said we would have to go this year that is from now until school is out April or May and some next winter so you see how awful long that would be. The reason is because it is in High School where if it were in some Business College it would not last more than 8 or 9 months at the most. They cannot devote much time to you in H. S. I have not heard from my land yet so cannot decide until I do, but I think it for the best to quit school and go to work and attend business college when I can even though I go unto my land, I'd rather have a piece of parcel home of my own than most anything. Dam the east anyway, with its narrow minded pernicious people.

I was at Waterloo yesterday, it is about 7 miles from here and I looked up a few places so if I decide to go to work, I'll know something. I think I'd rather wait tables as there is no expenses, while other work you haf to pay room and board and person cannot save anything that way.

I am surprised to hear of Pete N. having a boy. No wonder Laura was so fussy last summer, I should think she's felt like taking some people heads off, that told her how fat she was getting, but that accounts for it. Quite

Immigrants' Daughter

a Xmas present for Pete I should think. I am glad you like the mottos, I will fix up some prettier ones some day. Anna Reed sent me a very pretty handkerchief. I was rather surprised. How did Seth happen to get it into his head to go to Canada? I don't blame him for wanting to go there but I prefer Mont. I am glad he told whether he wanted to help me or not so I'd know but I feel that I ought not to give up that land and there is no reason why I can't hang onto it.

I guess I've written all I know. Write soon. I got some new button shoes, gunmetal leather. It is so much more serviceable than patent leather, especially for winter. Ma sent me $3. It certainly takes a lot for paper. You wouldn't think those little things would amount to much but they do, I only get 25 sheets type writing paper for 5 cents. Wish I could find some old devil that was about ready to croak that had about 50 thousand and was foolish enough to give it to me,

Write,

B.A.H.

At the beginning of this letter, she talks about drying her hair. As you can see from her pictures she has long, curly, blonde hair.

Why wouldn't her father want her to have a man of her own? Most farmers were trying to get their daughters, if they had any, married off, as it was far more desirable to have sons who could work in the fields. One of her nieces expressed that her father, too, was very strict and when I questioned if perhaps they were a religious family, she said no; perhaps it was simply a tradition from the old country.

The land she refers to is the parcel she has applied for in Montana (paperwork to follow in a later letter). Few single women had a desire or the knowledge to homestead a place of their own back then (or today either, for that matter). In fact, many young women were even denied basic schooling in the early 1900s, so Bessie taking courses to become a stenographer was highly unusual in itself.

Bessie does not seem to be swayed by the shoe styles of the day but more on their serviceability. Not many young beautiful women would choose gunmetal leather over patent leather.

Why is she so lonesome? Is she really going to high school as we would know it, or is she attending a different type of school? She would have been about 25 years old at the time of this letter, if the 1900 census was correct, and a little too old for high school. It does seem she is on her own more and just discovering the cost of things, like her comments about the writing paper.

Her statement "same address until I inform you different" is prophetic. Moving will become her lifestyle for many years to come.

Bessie and Esther
James Collection

Immigrants' Daughter
Herberg Family Tree

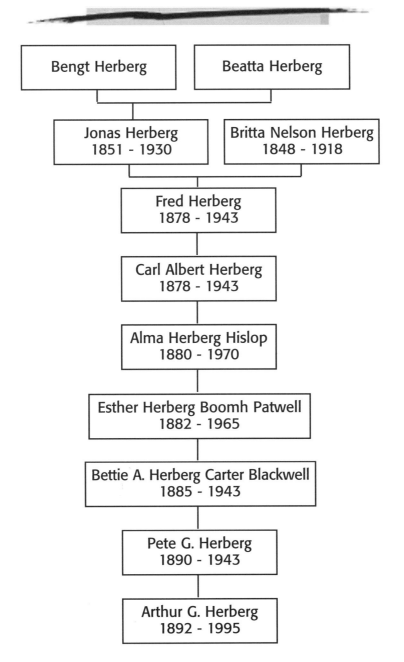

Bengt Herberg	Beatta Herberg

| Jonas Herberg 1851 - 1930 | Britta Nelson Herberg 1848 - 1918 |

Fred Herberg
1878 - 1943

Carl Albert Herberg
1878 - 1943

Alma Herberg Hislop
1880 - 1970

Esther Herberg Boomh Patwell
1882 - 1965

Bettie A. Herberg Carter Blackwell
1885 - 1943

Pete G. Herberg
1890 - 1943

Arthur G. Herberg
1892 - 1995

Chapter 2

Spreading Her Wings

Bessie
James Collection

Buckskin Bessie

Jan, 5, 1911
Cedar Falls, Iowa

Dear Sister,

You might as well write once in a while. I had a letter from Daddy. I did not know he had been having such a time with his side, he has been to Rochester and has not worked in his shop since I left. If I had known he had been having such hard luck I would have been back there before now, because Daddy has been better to me than anyone else ever has and any time he needs me I will sure come no matter where I am or what I am doing. I'm afraid he never will get wholly over it. It's where the horse kicked him in Billings after you left. I think perhaps that bullet he carried so long makes some difference. He says Kii is alright only a little thin. I think it is funny he got well because his leg was broke clean off every bone. I'll bet that happens only about one in a thousand.

Say, can you make me a plain white waist. I am going to do dining room work in Waterloo. I'm sure Ma will buy the goods. I want it just plain a few little tucks toward the shoulders and a square at the neck you know how I like it. I have black waists so I can get

along but need a white one for Sunday. They furnish
and laundry your aprons but all they pay is $22 ? per
week, but a nice up to date place. I am sure of the job
and think I can start work next week. Miss Dobry
my H. S. teacher says I can study my shorthand and
send her what I write and she will correct it for me. She
does not want me to quit school and I'm sure I don't
want to but I cannot see any other way out of it.

Can't give up that land no matter what comes.
Daddy said he had been getting letters from Seth.

Well I guess this is all, I would like that waist
awful well if you will make it as I cannot very well hire it
done because I'm broke.

I don't think it will cost more than 5 cents to send it
by mail.

B. A. H.

This letter poses so many questions. How many fathers do you
know who are carrying a bullet around inside? And of course, the
even bigger question…how did it get there?

Rochester, Minnesota, is a long distance from Ruthton, if that
is what she means. And what shop would he be working at if he is
homesteading?

I was never able to document who Kii is, but she mentions this
name a few different times.

Clearly she has not done a lot of sewing herself. She says she wants her waist (shirt) plain, with tucks and a square neck. In a 1920 United States Census report, it stated that Esther M. Boomh was 29 at that time and was listed as a power machine operator. Perhaps she was a seamstress? She seems to feel her sister is capable of making whatever she wants.

Having her own land seems to be something of a driving force for Bessie, and it will continue to be throughout the rest of her life. It probably should not be surprising, as the owning of land is what brought her parents to this country and gave them a new and prosperous life.

Why would she even think of hiring her waist made? Most women in this year of 1911 would never even imagine such a thing. This is another indication that Bessie may have come from a wealthier background than the average immigrant's daughter.

The following letter had no return address on it but it was postmarked from Montana.

Dear Folks,

Just received your letter and card and money, which comes in mighty handy to me at present time.

I rec'd a letter from Forest Dep't will enclose it in this. I am not going to relinquish my right. Have thought it over carefully and come to this conclusion. That piece of land is worth hanging onto in the first place you'd haf to hunt around a lot before you'd find another so close to town and it is on the reserve so grazing will never be scarce. The timber will be worth around $20.00 by the end of 5 years, cannot be sold until then. The meadow land can be drained, oats and wheat and potatoes grow fine

there. If you want to furnish the money, I will go onto it
and make a contract so that at the end of five years the haf
of it yours, regardless of what I can get for it then or I
will pay you during the 4 years and all the land be mine,
or you can have the stuff in your name, it be yours, and I
pay so much per month or 6 months.

I want 6 or 7 cows and a separator; it would take
$300 or $350. I imagine cows sell for $30 and $25 per
head. I would need a team and harness and some kind of
a rig, building. Building would not cost much. It would
be nice if you and Esther go there also and live there until
you decide on what you want. If I cannot raise the
money, I will hold it anyway; because I have a feeling
it is best to do so.

I expect I will haf to go there to file, but after that
would probably have 6 months. During that time I could
earn enough to make some improvements and live there a
while then work again and so on until my 5 yr. were up.
If I did that I would not have any stock only a few
horses that I could buy in the meantime. I might get
someone to do what I ask of you. I know Dr. Hall
would if he had the money. I think I will write Miss
Parson, she made me the proposition once, but she spoke of
her and me and another nurse all taking this land they keep

working and I take care of things. I do not see why she would not like this just as well, ? of it would be all she needed. There is another nurse I know that is working and saving her money for that purpose, but I don't think she has enough yet. Miss Parson has $600 saved up. I do not expect any help from Daddy as he is sore because I left there but I did not feel I was bettering conditions any.

I let Mr. Parsons read the letter from Forestry he said he did not like to advise anyone but if he were in my place he would not relinquish or at least get something for my right. He is a good financier. I do not know how much he is worth but he makes the money. Would not be surprised if he would buy the right for his boy, as he wants him to settle on a claim. But he is only a kid 20 so not very steady, a good boy though. But wants to see all the country he can and I do not blame him. I would haf to give up my shorthand, which I am sorry, for as I am making good headway, teachers say I am exceptionally good. But would haf to go to work at something so as to earn something in the time I had before going on. They pay good wages in the shirt factory here, 35 and 50 up to 65. I probably could get Arthur to come and stay a year of so or Roy, anyway, anyone so I would not have to stay alone.

Write me right away and tell me if you want to do anything so I will know just where I am at. I have written the Forestry that I want the land, so it's up to me to make good. I do not want you to do anything you do not feel alright in, as I want no afterward monkey business. I am old enough now or ought to be to know what I want. Nothing ventured, nothing gained. One fence would be all the place needed to keep the stock from getting away. Then the acres of 12-14 would haf to be fenced if I wanted to raise grain. I would need a shingled barn or something to keep wet out as milk cows need more care than do horses. I have one heifer coming in the spring.

The copy of the letter from the Forest Service follows. It is strange that she never mentions this land again, even though in this letter she says she has informed them she wants it and now would be required to make good on it. Bessie's life would have had a very different outcome had she homesteaded this land rather joining a Wild West Show.

Buckskin Bessie

(In this Forest Service letter, the name "Herberg" is misspelled.)

ADDRESS REPLY TO
"FOREST SUPERVISOR"

UNITED STATES DEPARTMENT OF AGRICULTURE
FOREST SERVICE
BEARTOOTH NATIONAL FOREST

Beartooth - Settlements
Herferg, Beatrice A., # 27.

RED LODGE, MONT.

December 12, 1910.

Miss Beatrice A. Herferg,

Cedar Falls, Iowa.

Dear Madam:-

From information recently received I understand
that you do not want the land applied for by you under the
Act of June 11, 1906. If this is the case I would be very
grateful to you if you would please write me a statement
addressed to the Forest Supervisor, Beartooth National Forest, to the effect that you do not care for the land.

Very truly yours,

Acting Forest Supervisor.

Armed with more than just a casual understanding about how to run a farm, she is very aware of all the things that are needed and about the homesteading laws and regulations. For instance, she's aware of having to make improvements on the land and not being able to sell any of it for five years. She is also very familiar with this particular parcel of land, including what will grow there and how much timber there is, etc.

Note that this land she speaks of in Red Lodge, Montana, would now, in the twenty-first century, be priceless. It is the gateway to Yellowstone National Park.

Bessie exhibits wisdom in seeking advice from someone she deemed wise in financial matters prior to making her decision.

How does she know these nurses and their personal business? Were they just friends or classmates or maybe they all roomed together?

You notice she calls Mr. Parson's son just a boy and he is 20. She herself was only about 25 or 26 years old at this time. Her interest in traveling is evident when she says, "I don't blame him for wanting to see all the country he can." Even in her wildest dreams, she would not have known how much country she would end up seeing herself, if only through the windows of a Pullman car.

THE IRVING HOTEL

C. L. KINGSLEY & M. H. KINGSLEY, Props.

WATERLOO, IOWA

Return if not called for in 5 days to

B. A. Herberg

Dear Esther,

I rec'd your letter. Am at the Irving doing dining room work. Like it well, but not very good wages 20 per. Get quite a few tips. I like Waterloo pretty well. About 28,000. Say if you've not started that waist do not bother as I will get along. I am sorry Ma does not feel well. This winter spose I ought to stay home but I'm not satisfied there.

I left my trunk at Parsons, but may get it after a

while. I am keeping up my studies. You see I have from 1:30 until quarter of 6. I have a dandy room, steam heated, water and electric light. Also telephone in my room. It didn't seem to bother me at all to start this kind of work. I am sleepy can hardly write,

B.A.H

Extra, Extra

The Irving hotel when it opened on June 17, 1884, ranked as one of the foremost hotels in the state and registered 10,000 guests in its first year. Three hundred invited guests attended the opening day festivities of the deluxe establishment, decked out with flowers and Christmas trees. The $5.00 per plate dinner, reflecting superb culinary artistry, included 13 meat entrees, a selection of ten deserts, not to mention other assorted and tantalizing accompaniments.

Photo courtesy of Leonard Katoski
Courtesy of Waterloo Convention & Visitors Bureau
Susan Lewis, Communication manager

Spreading Her Wings

April 16, 1911

Dear Sister,

Rec'd your card and will ans. this Easter afternoon. Say, I'm having some of them small pictures you
know Kodak pictures, enlarged because they are doing
them so reasonable, 48 cents a piece and are fine. I have
no good ones and want you to send me some that I sent
you. I will return them and maybe give you a couple of
the enlarged ones. I don't remember just what you have,
but remember one where I have men's clothing on and
Kii has his back turned, also one where I am in the
brush holding one horse and the other one is tied. And one
picture of Parsons and I where I am dressed as a
Mexican and she has my sombrero on. Then there was
me where we are in the corral and one where we are driving
the horses. You pick out all that are good and send them.
You need not be afraid of losing them for I will return
them as soon as I have some of them enlarged. Just send
them by mail and send them right away. I had the log
cabin enlarged and it is swell. So not know just when I
will come home but it will not be such a very long time.
Haf to earn a little more of the essential as I want a
new coat. I wish Seth would write to me.

Buckskin Bessie

I had a letter from J.C. Miller of the 101 Wild West Show. He wants me to ride for them. There is 30 per month to start with and expenses, but it is not pleasant traveling as you go in box cars and all that sort of thing.

Well, I guess I have said all I know. Write right away and send photos. You won't be sorry,

B.A.H.

This is a pivotal letter. She states that she received a letter from J.C. Miller of the 101 Wild West Show. There have been several books and documents written about the dynasty of 101 Ranch and Wild West Show owned by the Miller brothers, to which I will refer frequently, but the big question is, how did Joe Miller know Bessie? Joe Miller was from Ponca City, Oklahoma, where the Wild West show originated.

Here are a few possible scenarios:

(1). Bessie may have seen an advertisement for the Wild West Show and sent in an application to join. Maybe that is why she wants Esther to send her the pictures to have done.

(2). The famous couple, Vernon and Edith Tantlinger, who were already part of the 101 Wild West Show might have told Joe about her because Edith Tantlinger was a former school teacher from Pipestone, Minnesota, where Bessie and her family were from.[1]

(3). J.C. Miller could have stopped there at the hotel where Bessie was working, to either spend the night or have a meal during one of his many travels. One of the major rail lines went though there and he could have seen her working in the dining room. Joe Miller

[1] *The Real Wild West, pg. 307, Michael Wallis*

was always looking to recruit people for the Wild West Show. It was a huge operation with hundreds of employees. It was also known that Joe was a lady's man and it might have been that Joe was smitten with her from the very beginning.

Traveling in boxcars was very difficult and often times they functioned as their sleeping quarters as well. The 101 Ranch operated and owned their own trains and had 50 Pullmans and 100 freight cars.[2]

James Collection

Above is a replica of one of the Pullmans used and the longhorn steer seen on each end was one of the symbols associated with the 101. This may have been due to the report of the Millers having gathered up the longhorn steer, along with the buffalo, and bringing them to the ranch where they were well fed, bred, and rescued from extinction.[3]

There is, however, another version of this event and that is that they rounded them up for the sole purpose of making a huge impression for the first show they hosted at the ranch in June of 1904. Regardless, roaming buffalo and steer were always a part of the 101 Ranch.

Another contributing factor for the fame of these steer heads can be credited to Mr. Bill Picket (billed as "the Dusky Demon") who made

[2] *101 Ranch, pg. xii, Collins and England*
[3] *Ibid, pg. 164*

Buckskin Bessie

headlines with his steer wrestling skill, plummeting steers whose horns were said to have been between six and seven feet wide.[4]

And yet another famous steer head will become well known but this one will have diamond eyes.

[4] *The Real Wild West, pg. 256, Michael Wallis*

Chapter 3

Joined the Show

Bessie
Courtesy of Judy Roberts

Buckskin Bessie

April 1911
The Irving Hotel
Waterloo, Iowa

Dear Sister,

Well I'm going East. Start tonight for Baltimore, the 101 Wild West Show sent me ticket, Maybe I am not doing the correct thing but I do not haf to stick if it is not satisfactory.

I don't know what you can tell the folks because you could never convince them it was alright. I think you had better keep it to yourself for a while until I see how I like it. But use your own judgment. I suppose you could say that I had position as ladies maid or companion. You know that is pretty good job and it would not seem funny that my letters came from different towns because lots of wealthy women travel like that.

I rec'd photos but cannot do anything with them at present time because I will not be here but I shall certainly have them fixed up for you. I sent a box of stuff to you, I cannot lug so much stuff around. There is some shirt waist goods for Ma.

The rest of the stuff you can have, all but my coat. The hat will be mashed but the beaver will be just as good. Think you can have a winter hat made from it. I have *worn it 2 winters so am tired of it now. Do not worry about me going so far because you know I am capable of holding my own. I go by way of Chi- go not feel like leaving here so very much as I have made some might good friends, but am so tired of dining room work. I will not work inside in summer. I did not pay freight on box as I wanted all the money I could get, because a person never knows what may happen. I'll write soon as I am located.*

Your Sister,
B. A. H

It seems she made this decision to join the Wild West Show not knowing what it would be like or even knowing anyone there. This is more than just a little adventurous! A few of the deciding factors seemed to be that she would no longer have to stay indoors in the summertime and that she was tired of waitress work. She also was under the impression that she could change her mind and come home. Her life, however, was forever changed by this one decision. There would be no turning back.

Traveling light would have to become an art for the many years ahead.

Indeed, she is old enough to make her own decisions, but a single woman joining a circus was not a claim to fame but rather regarded as a pending disaster by her parents. She shows her concern for them in her desire to not disappoint them or worry them.

Bessie had a very close relationship with her sister Esther, and she confides in her often. There were also a few letters in the packet that were written to Esther from her other siblings and it seems that Esther was a bit of glue for the Herberg family.

Buckskin Bessie

April 27, 1911
Trenton, N. J.

Dear Sister,

Well, I went with the 101. We are moving tonight. Go to Brooklyn New York. Will be there one week so if you write right away I will get it. Have you said anything to the folks about it? If you haven't done it yet you'd better not, as I do not think I will stay as it is too hard for the money there is in it, but will have to stick with it for a while to pay back my fare.

Well, I'll haf to cut this short, will write again tomorrow if I have time.

B. A. H

A 1911 Wild West show roster can be found on the following web site: www.kaycounty.info/101_Ranch/1911-101wws.htm

This roster lists around 340 people that were a part of the show at that time, including our very own Bessie Herberg. No wonder she felt a bit lost. True with most jobs in life, there was a lot more to it than what it appeared at first. Just being part of the show, looking pretty, and riding your horse in the parade were but a small part compared to all of the hard work behind the scenes. That is probably why she says, "it is too hard for the money." Also, you will note that she is required to pay her fare back that they had sent ahead for her to come on board. It should be noted that the age old saying, "There are no free rides" is true.

Joined The Show

April 29, 1911
Newark, N. J.

Dear Sister,

Well, I've done most everything that anyone does in the circus and like it very much, but it's hard work for the money. Only 30 per month but I will get more than that after a while or I won't stay.

Spose Ma will think I am crazy but this is a circus anyone need not be ashamed of. All nice girls, no swearing or anything rough, we are not allowed to monkey around with the boys at all, It could not be stricter. Mr. Miller is certainly a nice man, he is the owner of the 101 Show. You know about this show don't you, it's really a better one than Buffalo Bills. Say if you think we had better not tell the folks about it, I can write and mail the letters to you or mail them on the train, you know we could never convince Ma that circus life is decent. As a rule or lots of times the girls are tough. Now write me right away and I'll get it next week. Send everything c/o 101 Wild West Show.

B.A.. H.
Brooklyn N. York for a week

Her statement, "Well, I've done most everything that anyone does in the circus" was a bit odd as there were literally hundreds of different types of jobs involved to make the show a success—from the people whose job it was to create the route for the season to those who traveled ahead of the show and made all the huge posters that advertised their coming. There were people whose job it was to unload and set up the tents, arena and grandstands to people who cared for the animals and those who worked in the cookhouse that had to be ready to feed hundreds of people at the drop of hat, and even the seamstresses who created outfits and did repairs along the way. I am sure she was not required to work in all of those different areas but without question, hard work was required by all.

True to what seems to be her nature, she has adjusted in a flash of time and is looking to the future possibilities. You notice she used the term "stricter"? Since her father was known to be so strict, maybe she saw this as a good thing, something that offered protection and rightness and perhaps one of the contributing factors to her feeling comfortable to stay. For others, however, their perspective of Joe Miller's "strictness" was simply that he was being controlling. The Miller brothers were very powerful and many felt their actions seemed to follow the theory that the end justified the means.

It is notable that she says "Mr. Miller does not allow any monkey business with the boys," and yet it is his heart that she eventually captures and he pursues her even in the face of great personal loss.

Joe Miller
Stevens Collection

Chapter 4

The 101 Ranch & The Wild West Show

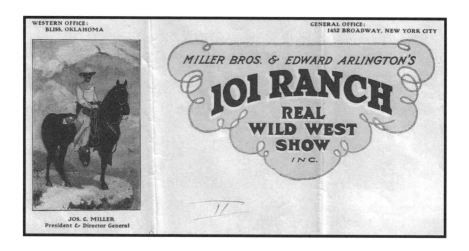

Buckskin Bessie

The fame of the 101 Ranch and the Wild West Show has already been well documented.

I simply will recap some known facts about these two empires.

The 101 Ranch was established in the late 1800s by George Washington Miller and grew to include leased land from four different Indian tribes: the Ponca, Otoe, Pawnee, and Osage and covered the Oklahoma counties of Kay, Noble, Osage, and Pawnee, all located along the Salt Fork River.

This growth is credited to not only George Miller and his wife Molly, but also to their surviving children:

Joe. C. Miller, the farmer and show man

Zack T. Miller, the livestock man

George L. Miller, the banker and lawyer

Alma Miller, the historian

The ranch grew to become a 110,000-acre, self-contained city that supplied not only itself, but far-reaching territories with beef, poultry, milk and milk products, and later, oil. Mail was delivered daily by mounted riders and vast amounts of people flocked there for the opportunity to experience the real west through the graciousness of this expansive ranch. In fact, it was documented that nearly 65,000 people attended the first show held at the 101 Ranch in 1905[1] and the Riverside Camp that was established years later may have been the first guest ranch facility created.[2]

What it must have been like to behold the "White House" that cost $35,000 to build in the year of 1909,[3] the silos, and the Indian tepees scattered throughout, the bunkhouses, and the two-story grocery store that supplied everything from sewing needles to a new car, and the local café that offered everything fresh from eggs to homemade pies, the buffalo and the longhorn steer that freely roamed, and last but not least, the fields and fields of crops. "In 1923, the (garden) consisted of 125,000 Bermuda onion plants, 400 acres of Irish potatoes, 25,000 frost-proof cabbage plants, 6,000 tomato plants, 160

---

[1] *The Real Wild West,* pg. 249, Michael Wallis
[2] *101 Ranch,* pg. 159, Collins and England
[3] *The Real Wild West,* pg. 338, Michael Wallis

acres of sweet potatoes, 30 acres of cantaloupes, 200 acres of watermelon and muskmelons, 200 acres of peanuts, and 25 acres of corn for roasting ears" and lastly 75,000 acres of wheat.[4]

James Collection

This was not the entirety of it, but it gives you an idea of the vastness of their agricultural operation. They produced thousands of eggs and processed 100 hogs and 50 head of cattle each day. They had their own tannery and supplied not only themselves with saddles, harnesses, and tack, but others as well. To add to the picture were the oil fields that were steadily pumping oil from 1923 to 1930 and bringing in $190,000.00 annually.[5]

[4] *101 Ranch, pg. XIV, Collins and England*
[5] *Ibid, pg. 111*

Buckskin Bessie

Stevens Collection

Not only could they afford to be their own boss, but they controlled their future as well, maintaining their own churches and schools and paying their employees with 101 printed money. The success of these two empires was due to the diversity of the talents of the three brothers that were left to run it after their father's death in 1903, and each of them contributed equally.

The 101 Wild West Show got its roots from the Miller's desire to influence their Oklahoma territory by creating a newspaper called the Bliss Breeze which in turn led them to rub shoulders with members of the National Editorial Association at a convention held in Saint Louis in 1904.[6] It was there that the Millers boldly made an offer to host a Wild West show at their ranch in exchange for the next convention to be held in Oklahoma. A "buffalo chase" roundup show was held at the ranch as a dress rehearsal for the show that was to take place in June of 1905. The thirst for the roar of the crowd was immediately sparked. The visions of a Wild West show came to fruition and were adorned with bands, sharp-shooting acts, and rodeo acts such as trick riding and championship equestrian events. Also included were Indian villages with the Native Americans doing

[6] *The Real Wild West, pg. 217, Michael Wallis*

their traditional songs, dances, and ceremonies,[7] and Western-themed dramas that showed the spectators vivid visions of the real Western life. Recreations of historical events, like the "Pat Hennessey Massacre,"[8] and an exhibition of the Pony Express were all performed in an arena tent that measured 390 feet in width by 550 feet in length.[9] Add to that the more than 600 elephants, camels, horses, buffalo, longhorn steer, oxen, mules, and ponies and some of the most beautiful Wild West women you would ever want to see. Is it any wonder that people from around the world flocked to see them as they toured from one end of the United States to the other?

From the fall of 1908 to the fall of 1916, the Wild West shows made a net profit of over $800,000.[10]

Written on the back: "I (Bessie) am supposed to be a squaw and Orrie a papoose and the lady is preacher's wife."

James Collection

---

[7] *Life in the Wild West,* pg. 24, Steven Currie
[8] *Ibid* pg. 28
[9] *101 Ranch,* pg. 175, Collins and England
[10] *101 Ranch,* pg. 186, Collins and England

Chapter 5

On the Road

Bessie with Edith and Vernon Tantlinger
Stevens Collection

Extra, Extra

The following newspaper clipping surfaced while doing research and since this chapter picture is of Bessie with the Tantlingers, I had to include it.

Sheboygan Press
Sheboygan, Wisconsin
April 13, 1912
Venice, Ca.

Vernon Tantlinger, a boomerang thrower attached to one of the shows wintering here, is bagging ducks without violating the Ordinance. His skill with the boomerangs enables him to take ducks without "exploding firearms within the limits of the city."

This morning on the oceanfront he got twelve nice plump ducks.

His mode is to send one of the boomerangs into a flock of swimming ducks and when they rise he is prepared to scale another while they are bunched on the wing. The incoming tide floats both the ducks and the boomerang back to him.

May 8, 1911
Brooklyn, N. Y.

Dear Sister,

I re'c your letter yesterday so you've not told. I am glad of it, not that it is anything to be ashamed of, just the opposite but Ma would worry and you cannot convince them it is alright. Who do you suppose I saw?

On The Road

You remember the New York boys, Billy and Freddie? Well the day we rode into the show grounds there stood Billy. He said he was not so very surprised, he brought his Mother to the show and I had dinner at their home. Gee but they have a swell place, she served a course dinner. She is certainly a dandy woman. Just as jolly as a girl, was crazy about the show and 1 day we are going out in automobile to see Prospect Park. Then this afternoon Freddie wants me to take dinner with him but am afraid I can't as we are leaving.

Billy is starting for R. Lodge Tues. he won't tell Daddy that he saw me as I think it would worry him not that he'd be surprised, because Billy told me, that Daddy told him to look for me in Buffalo Bills show. I don't know why, because I have never even thought of such a thing. Say, that's just the correct thing to tell the folks because they employ stenographers and you can put my letters c/o The Miller Bros. Don't need to put "Wild West" on it at all but put my full name because I may not get it otherwise. I do not intend to stay with this so very long. We will hit Billings about August I think. I will get a route card so you can write whenever you want to. I'll bet Ma's davenport is nice at that price. Say, I saw a dining room papered in tan plain with a wide grape border.

Well, I guess it's time for me to close. I wish I had my good saddle here but of course I cannot send for it as Daddy would know.

Write me at Meriden, Conn. That is the next Saturday town so your letter will have plenty of time to reach me. Then you can see the Route card for the next week in Mass.

Extra, Extra

Prospect Park is a 526-acre park located in Brooklyn and still enjoyed today, hosting free outdoor concerts in the summertime and various sports and fitness activities.

Allen Collection

As seen from this route card, they kept a grueling schedule, moving almost every day to a different location and each time,

OFFICIAL ROUTE CARD No. 2

MILLER BROS.
& ARLINGTON

101 Ranch

REAL
WILD
WEST
INC.

GEORGE ARLINGTON
GENERAL MANAGER
JOS. C. MILLER ·
EDW. ARLINGTON ·
GEO. L MILLER ·
Z. T MILLER ·
EQUAL OWNERS.
FRED BECKMANN
GEN'L AGENT

DATE			TOWN	STATE	R R	MILES
4TH WEEK						
Mon.,	May	1	Brooklyn	N. Y.	P R R	12
Tues.,	"	2	"	"	Bush Terminals	
Wed.,	"	3	"	"		
Thurs.,	"	4	" Show Grounds	"		
i.,	"	5	" 5th Ave. &	"		
Sat.,	"	6	" 3rd St.	"		
5TH WEEK						
Mon.,	May	8	Hartford	Conn.	Bush Terminals–NYNH&H	113
Tues.,	"	9	Waterbury	"	N Y. N H & H	32
Wed.,	"	10	Bridgeport	"	"	33
Thurs.,	"	11	Ansonia	"	"	16
Fri.,	"	12	New Haven	"	"	13
Sat.,	"	13	Meriden	"	"	19
6TH WEEK						
Mon.,	May	15	Worcester	Mass.	N Y N H & H–B & A	109
Tues.,	"	16	Brockton	"	B & A–N Y N H & H	64
Wed.,	"	17	Providence	R. I.	N Y N H & H	48
Thurs.,	"	18	"	"	"	
Fri.,	"	19	Norwich	Conn.	N Y N H & H	76
Sat.,	"	20	New London	"	"	14

only one day *These places* *will go this place* *this coming wk.*

GENERAL OFFICES. 1432 BROADWAY.
NEW YORK CITY

everything had to be taken down, packed up, and loaded into the boxcars and then set up all over again.

It's difficult to comprehend the magnitude of that task until you read some of the details that were involved: "crew members set up a large heavy canvas for a side wall....10 to 12 feet in height. That wall used up five thousand yards of canvas. Covering the grandstand required seven thousand more."[1] And that was a mere beginning of all that would be needed—tents for the dining rooms and sleeping quarters, all the props that were required for the show, and the multitude of lights that were run by portable generators, not to mention all that was required to care for the animals. This required supremacy in organization.

She states that her father is in Red Lodge, so that must have been who she was with back in the very first letter she wrote in 1907. Again, it seems that her mother was not there with them. I have questioned family members whether Bessie's parents were ever separated or divorced. They all said no, they didn't think so.

July 24, 1911
Benton Harbor, Mich.

Dear Sister,

I haven't heard from you for a long time but I suppose you have run out of route cards. If at any time you haven't my address and want me real bad, you can put it c/o Billboard Cincinnati, Ohio, 101 W.W. Show.

I am getting along fine. Am riding a high school horse now, a big black mare. She certainly is pretty.

[1] *Life in a Real Wild West Show*, pg. 62, Steven Currie

On The Road

She cake walks, marches, dances and lot of other steps.

How are the folks? It's possible this show may go to Minneapolis. You ought to be able to come and see me then. Today it's raining but we are going to show. Have showed the last 2 Sundays. We were in Chicago 8 days but I did not go to see J. Albert. I have his address but he lives way out. Another girl and I went to hunt friends of hers. We had the address but the streetcar conductor told us wrong so we did not have time to look further. If you have plenty of time you can easily find anyone. It certainly has been warm, don't know how I stood it as I'm not used to such hot weather but I did better than most of the girls. What is Seth doing now? I had another letter from Billy, he says money is scarce in the West. He takes camping parties out makes good money. Says Daddy cannot ride any yet. Dear old Daddy, how I miss him if he only wasn't so strict I would stay there all the time, for he needs me more than anyone. I am glad that Ma pays lot and gets good things little by little she will have the house furnished. I would like to have the stuff and fix the hall upstairs. Well, I guess I will close.

Write soon, B.A.H

Extra, Extra

According to the Merriam-Webster Dictionary, a cake-walk is a stage dance developed from walking steps and figures typically involving a high prance with a backward tilt.

A "high school horse" was a highly trained horse. One of the equestrian displays for the show was described in A.K. Greenland's writing in the Billboard dated August 15, 1911, as "having a number of well trained high school horses and climaxed by the famous Madame Marantette" act.[2]

RETURN, IF NOT CALLED FOR IN FIVE DAYS, TO
MENDON, MICHIGAN

MADAM MARANTETTE
EQUESTRIENNE QUEEN
WILL COMPETE FOR $2,000 AGAINST ANY LADY
RIDER OR DRIVER IN THE WORLD

The above picture on the return envelope was a woman who had such a high status that her train car was the only one painted white as they headed west.[3]

The following story was shared by Betty Allen, who is Bessie's niece:

My Dad told me that when Bessie was young before she left home, their neighbor came rushing over to my grandfather Jonas

---

[2] *The 101 Ranch,* pg. 177, Collins and England
[3] *The Real Wild West,* pg. 357, Michael Wallis

and told him that his hired man was crazy, he was standing on top of the horses jumping around and my grandfather said, "No, that is not a hired man, it's my daughter Bettie. She was plowing and would always get on the horses and dance."

Bessie's fancy horse-riding days started in those open fields of Minnesota.

Rain, wind, snow, or sunshine the show went on. The spectators were normally protected under the canvas top, but this was not so with the performers.

There was no date on the following letter but it is postmarked from Minneapolis.

Dear Sister,

We are in Mps. today, got here yesterday. Have not seen anyone I know. Rained today but had a big house. I have a girl friend coming on here. Think we will close in Texas. Will go to Oklahoma after leaving here. I thought you told the folks I was traveling around. You had better or they will be surprised when I write from some other place. Had a letter from Billy. Says Bill Grevisugh is dead. You remember Wright his brother?

Daddy is working now. Have not written them yet.

Well, I guess this is all. Mr. Miller took us to a swell play last night.

Write soon,
B. A. H.

Buckskin Bessie

Ethel and Juanita Parry, Joe Miller, Bessie Herberg
Stevens Collection

It is possible that this picture was taken at one of the many Fred Harvey Houses that serviced and populated the railways during this time. Most had beautiful courtyards similar to this one, and in Edith Tanglinger's diary[4] she documents staying at one of them.

When the season ended, many of the performers went back to the 101 Ranch and recuperated while working there through the winter. According to this letter, this was Bessie's plan (but this did not happen due to the decision to winter in Los Angeles.[5]) Injuries while touring were commonplace, so recuperation was often needed. Even though the work on the ranch was laborious, it was not filled with the danger they faced daily in the shows.

[4] *Edith Tantlinger Diary, University of Oklahoma Library, Western History Collection, Norman, Oklahoma*
[5] *The Real Wild West, pg. 357, Michael Wallis*

On The Road

> **Extra, Extra:**
> The members of the show were required to sign a contract that not only governed their conduct but it was common procedure that you would be required to pay your own funeral expense if you died.6 Each shows contract varied.

From Prince Albert, Canada

Dear Sister,

This is our last town in Can. I am not sorry. Although I like Canada pretty good now. Everything is late but I guess they don't have any trouble in getting things ripe. Great range country, lots of grass. Did Seth give up the idea of going there? We will be getting pretty close to you. Does anyone know I am with the show? Spose I'll run into someone I know. Did I tell you I ran into Harvey Pattern in some town in Cal. think it was Los Angeles. Said he knew me on parade. Invited me out to dinner at his mothers but I could not go as there were so many people I knew and it's an effort to talk to him because he is so deaf. I had a letter from Wilson, said daddy had not came home. Do not know how his mother is. Orrie has grown quite a bit.

6 *Buffalo Bill and the Enduring West, pg. 79, Hall from Prince Albert Canada*

Buckskin Bessie

He is certainly a good youngster, rides any place now and does most everything. Guess I will sell my horses. Both for $150. They are worth more than that, but do not like to monkey with them.

Guess this is all. Have not heard from Amy lately. Guess I told you I met Grandma and G. Pa Hislop at Everett. Mr. Hislop brought me a box of strawberries he raised. Don't think Laura was there or she would have seen me in parade as I am very noticeable. You get that. Believe me I have some saddle now, you know how nice my old one was, this one is way ahead of that one. Write,

Bessie

This is the first letter we see her sign "Bessie." It is not known how she got this nickname (maybe from Joe Miller), but it is the name she will carry to her grave.

Orrie is the boy dressed as an Indian in a picture with Bessie on page 45.

Amy Hislop is her sister and she was married to Fred Hislop. Grandma and Grandpa Hislop would have been her sisters in-laws. It appears that they were in Everett, Washington.

Bessie
Stevens Collection

Although difficult to see, this is the fancy tooled leather saddle with very large silver pieces on it. Just as in the many pictures of Joe Miller's saddle, it probably does not begin to show the beauty of it, but this was a gift from Joe Miller[7] and was to have matched his with the many pieces of silver, gold, and precious stones.

Even though she is traveling all over the world with all its sights and sounds, her attention is always drawn to the land and the crops. "You can take the girl out of the county but you cannot take the country out of the girl."

[7] *The Real Wild West, pg. 429 Michael Wallis*

Buckskin Bessie

Copy of envelope:

New Hotel St. Mark

150 ROOMS——100 WITH BATHS

SUPPLIED WITH

HOT AND COLD, FRESH AND SALT WATER

STEAM HEAT, ELEVATOR

ANDREW S. LEE, PROPRIETOR

Copy of the letterhead on stationery on which the letter was written:

This hotel is where the 101 stayed while wintering in Los Angeles after completing their grueling 7½ month road tour of 1911.[8]

Dec. 1911

Venice, Calif.

Dear Sister,

   Rec'd your letter and I don't think it worth while to send that trunk. We will send you the key and you

[8] *The Real Wild West, pg. 358, Michael Wallis*

can wear that red serge dress of mine. There is a silk petticoat to match it and any thing else of mine in trunk you can wear you are welcome to. I think you will know Minnie's and my stuff apart. I have a pretty vase in there also. Better let Ma use it as she has my cut glass one. This is a grand country to winter in. I am dressed same as if it were summer. We have a room at the St. Marks, are not showing but posing for moving pictures for the Bison people. It is certainly a snap. I get small wages now, $8 per wk. And cost quite a bit to live, but did not figure on making anything but expenses and one or two riding habits. Guess this is all so will close.

Write, B.A.H.

In *The Real Wild West* written by Michael Wallis, a full section was devoted to the movie people "Bison 101" and I quote from page 366, "Our arrangement gave us the use of about seventy-five cowboys and about thirty-five Indians and their squaws, who spoke no English. One of the tribe, a rather fat squaw who called herself Minnie was their teacher and interpreter."

In picture below, a large Indian lady at the end of the row is probably the Minnie that Bessie spoke of in this letter. She is a lot larger than Bessie and would account for the ease in being able to tell the difference in whose things belonged to whom.

Buckskin Bessie

Left to right: Unknown, the Parry twins, Martha Allen,
Bessie and perhaps the Minnie mentioned above.
Bob White Collection

The winter weather was great, the work was easy and clean, and they were not on the move constantly. They were often treated with movie star status, so it was not hard to understand why she would settle for smaller wages.

Their riding habits were of great importance and for some, like Bessie, a claim to fame (thus, her show name of Buckskin Bessie), even though her pictures do not always show her wearing a type of buckskin. Her other alias ("Montana Bess") could be due to her choice of hat known as a Montana peak. Large hats seemed to be the order of the day and almost obscured the person whose head it rested on.

Jan 1912
Venice, California

Dear Sister,
Say, Minnie wants the trunk sent on as soon as

possible by freight. I thought of another waist, a white one you can also take out, I guess you'll know. It's new has not been laundered and quite fancy. Be sure and take out the vase. I won the relay race at Pasadena. Can't find a paper to send, did not give us a very big write up, but would have like to sent you one. I mailed you a photograph yesterday, hope you get it alright. Send the trunk to Minnie Thompson, Venice, Cal.

   Had a letter from Daddy's they are getting along alright I guess. Mrs. Wilson is with them. She used to be there when I was some times. She's lots of help, likes horses and can do any work a man can. I may get one of my horses and saddle when we get somewhere near there this spring. I wrote to Annie. To bad Alma is sick so much. Guess I have written enough.

Write,

B.A.H.

   Winning the relay race was not an easy task. It was a grueling ten-mile event in which each of the four riders used five horses, changing mounts every one-half mile. She must have been disappointed that there was not a large write-up when in fact after one of her fellow competitors won, there was a huge article in the *San Francisco Chronicle*.[9] This was the fate of being part of the show and whatever tickled the fancy of the audience for the night drew the attention.

9 *The Real Wild West*, pg. 428, Michael Wallis

Buckskin Bessie

The following letter is to Esther from Minnie in the year of 1913:

HOTEL JEFFERSON

OBION, TENNESSEE

1/16 1913

Dear Mrs Boehm,

Your letter red and certainly thank you in being so prompt. Mrs Boehm I have decided having my trunk sent Express as I am in a hurry to get it here. so please send it Cod. and if possible send it Via St Paul as it will be nearer If there has been any expense draying or such on my trunk please let me know and I shall send it to you Thanking you many times for all your trouble.

Yours Minnie Thompson
Obion Tenn.
Gen Del.

On The Road

Written on the back of this picture: This was taken day of the race
I won at Pasadena. The tall man in this picture had a flying machine.
He came from Panama; don't know how long he was on the road.
The other fellow is Mr. Brooks, Mr. M. cousin.

James Collection

It should be noted that Mr. Brooks (above) was William A. Brooks and much more than just a cousin to the Miller brothers. He was the assistant manager of the Wild West Show[10] and eventually a trustee of the entire Miller brother's estate.[11] It is believed that the woman next to Bessie is her good friend, Martha Allen.

[10] *1911 101 Wild West Roster*
[11] *The Real Wild West, pg. 467, Michael Wallis*

Buckskin Bessie

Their time spent here in Pasadena was during the Tournament of Roses where they marched in the Rose Parade[12] but Bessie makes no mention of it in her letter home.

Either Bessie herself was not very impressed with all the world events or she did not feel the need to impress her sister with them.

March 29, 1912
Pasadena, Calif.

Dear Sister,

Well, we are on the road again. Started last Sunday. I think after all I like the moving pictures the best as we have nice rooms and baths. I may not stay with show all summer but never can tell. We will go near Red Lodge, show at Billings. I may take my horses on. How is everything at home? Arthur never does write to me. Had a letter from Amy a couple of wks ago, also from Daddy's. Folks there have three ft. of snow there. I guess they are going to leave for a while, Daddy has some kind of a contract, don't know what it is. Mrs. Wilson says they have all got ski's. Orrie can go on them fine, says she went to town on them. This is an awful pretty town so many flowers and orange trees. This

12 *The Real Wild West, pg. 360, Michael Wallis*

On The Road

is the town where I won the relay race. Well I guess this is all,

Write,

Your Sister,

B.A. H.

(An enclosed handwritten schedule)

Mon.	Apr,	1.	Anaheim, Cal.
Tues.	"	2.	San Diego "
Wed.	"	3.	Escondido "
Thurs.	"	4.	Escondido "
Fri.	"	5.	Corona "
Sat.	"	6.	Redlands "
Mon.	"	8.	Bakersfield "
Tues.	"	9.	Taft "
Wed.	"	10.	Hanford Cal. "
Thurs.	"	11.	Visalia "
Fri.	"	12.	Fresno "
Sat.	"	13.	Merced "

Ah, the key to most women's hearts...a nice room and a bath. But then the grueling road tour started again. The show performed every single day without a break from April 1st to May 11th.[13]

Bessie shows great diligence in trying to maintain a relationship

---

[13] *The Real Wild West*, pg. 389, Michael Wallis

with her family in spite of the constant moving. She often makes note of whom she has heard back from and clearly anticipates those letters that keep her in touch with home.

Whoever Orrie is, he is with her father and Mrs. Wilson now.

It is not known what is meant by a contract, but it may have something to do with the fact that if you left the land on which you made a claim, you could lose it.

Extra, Extra:
The world was thrown into a state of shock at the sinking of the Titanic that killed over 1,500 people on April 14, 1912, occurring less than one month after the above letter.

James Collection

[14] *Edith Tantlinger Diary, University of Oklahoma Library, Western History Collection, Norman, Okla.*

On The Road

Edith Tantlinger[14] meticulously logged daily events in her diary and on May 12, 1912, it was written "Bessie Herberg left to go home to Red Lodge, Montana for a few days visit"—that follows the time line for Bessie's letter below.

Hello Esther,

Put on your glad rags and come to Sioux Falls. Annie is with me and I don't like to send her on alone. She came along from Wapheton. Alma and Fred and Etheleen came to see me and I thought it would be a nice trip for her and she sure wanted to go. Of course she can go to Ruthton alone but it would be much nicer for her if you would come and I think you would enjoy seeing the show, write on wire so we will know.

As Ever,

B.A.H.

Bring suitcase as she has a couple dresses etc.

Alma was her older sister and Fred was Alma's husband. Etheleen was her niece, as well as Annie (above).

Bessie loved her nieces and often had them come and visit her while with the show.

Buckskin Bessie

No letter was found inside this envelope but the date of July 10, 1912, was very clear.

MEDICINE HAT, ALBERTA.

Extra, Extra:
This hotel is now known as the Assiniboia Inn. The original building burnt down around 1964.

Information courtesy of Grant Rombough, Medicine Hat, Alberta, Canada.

Aug. 17, 1912
Bryan, Ohio

Dear Sister,

Yours rec'd. Could not imagine why you did not write. I thought I sent you route before you came on. I bet Amy won't forget her visit. The weather has been

On The Road

quite warm since you left. You know the season is more than half over. I am not sorry, have no idea where we will close. Last Fri. morning 3 o'clock we had a terrible wreck. 4 stock cars ran off the track and 9 horses were trampled to death before they could be gotten out, 5 of the baggage horses and 4 arena horses. There were three horses laying on Anna Marks, but she came out pretty good. She is skinned up pretty bad. Had to drag them all out with ropes and block & tackle on the baggage horses. They chopped the roof out of the car Anna was in. It certainly was an awful sight. My saddle did not get hurt enough to do any harm. I got it out myself. I never saw a mess like that before. Hope I never will again but we are lucky it wasn't our sleeper.

Mr. M. has returned and he brought the gray leather bag so will send it to you. The photographer kept it as he did not know just where to send it. I am going to make a brown one for Annie. Ask Ma if she wants one. How is everything at home?

Hope you left a good impression with Ma.

Guess this is all. Write,

As Ever B.A. H

Buckskin Bessie

Train crashes were part of the danger of traveling with the show. This particular crash was indeed a bad one and it was reported, "No human lives were lost, but five valuable area horses including a roan bucking, bronco, and five team horses were killed and thirty horses were injured."[15]

She now refers to Joe Miller as Mr. M. Perhaps as his titles change, so does their relationship. Joe Miller was about 47 years old when he began this relationship with Bessie, 20 years his junior. He was married with two children. His wife and children, however, lived in Ponca City and not on the ranch, and they did not maintain a close relationship from 1907 until they finally divorced in 1917.[16] It was public knowledge that Joe was a lady's man but never before had he had more than a casual fling until he met his match in Miss Bessie Herberg.

She mentions a visit from her two sisters, Amy and Esther, and an opportunity for them to see her in the show. This no doubt was a memorable time for them all.

The gray leather bag she speaks of may have been a type of photo album and she is making it especially for them.

Nov. 6, 1912
Hot Springs, Ark.
Dear Sister,

Well, today is our last stand. Part of the show winters here, some go to Venice and a few to the ranch. Parry girls, Martha and I are going to the ranch. I am going to play there 4 or 5 wks. Then I do not know exactly what I am going to do but have a chance to go on a trip to Hawaiian Island with Mr. Miller &

---

[15] *The Real Wild West*, pg. 391, Michael Wallis
[16] *Ibid*, Pg. 289

party. Guess I ought to go, as I may never have
another chance. We had another big wreck, several flats
and a couple of bandwagons smashed. No one hurt much.

    I expected to hear from you before now. Not had
a letter for a long time. Write me at Bliss, Okla.
c/o 101 Ranch

                              Write Soon B.

They sometimes continued to do show work on the ranch to
entertain different personal guests and to make movies there. There
are many references to "Martha" in the letters which continues to
substantiate that she and Bessie were very good friends.

Dec. 1912
101 Ranch

Dear Sister,

    Rec'd your card and handkerchief it was pretty. I
am going on that long looked for trip in a few days. I
want you to forward letters for me as I do not want the
girls to know where I go. They think I went to see you
so I will write to them a few times, enclose the letters in
yours and you can send them on. Their postmark will be
Ruthton and they will still think I am there. If they

knew about this trip they would be sore, and say I had better stand in than they had which might be true but it wouldn't do to let them know that. There are five of us going. I will write to you right along and tell you where a letter will reach me. Don't know myself yet. I think we are going East instead of West, were going to Hawaiian Island but don't know if we will go there or not. Hope you had a nice Xmas. Give Seth my best. Will write soon as I can. Start Jan. 2nd I think.

Though there was not much written about the relationship between Bessie and Joe until around 1915, unquestionably this was the reason she "had a better stand in" as she says. Take special notice as to how she has arranged for letters to go to one place when she was indeed in another place. This is just the beginning of this practice so that her and Joe could be together without others knowing.

Chapter 6

The Trip

SS Kaiser Wilhelm II (German Passenger Steamship, 1903)

Buckskin Bessie

The following letter was written on a train en route to New York to begin a trip overseas.

Form 2289 T.

NIGHT LETTER

THE WESTERN UNION TELEGRAPH COMPANY
INCORPORATED
25,000 OFFICES IN AMERICA   CABLE SERVICE TO ALL THE WORLD

THEO. N. VAIL, PRESIDENT   BELVIDERE BROOKS, GENERAL MANAGER

RECEIVER'S No.	TIME FILED	CHECK

SEND the following NIGHT LETTER subject to the terms on back hereof, which are hereby agreed to   191

TO

Jan, 1913

Dear Sister,

I am in the train going through Virginia. We reach Washington DC tonight 12 o'clock. Don't know if you can read this or not the train shakes so. This is beautiful country. Mts, something like Mont. Only mts. much smaller. It's just like spring. The grass has started to grow. This is certainly grand trip so far. We get to N. York 7 in the morning.

                            As Ever, B.A.H.

Picture on an envelope dated, January 21, 1913, and postmarked from Times Square Station N.Y. with no letter inside. Bessie must have saved this envelope from a previous engagement in Oklahoma City.

The Trip

Hotel Kingkade

OKLAHOMA CITY, OKLA.,

James Collection

NAVARRE HOTEL   WRITING ROOM   SEVENTH AVE. AT 38TH ST., NEW YORK

Did Bessie sit in this writing room to pen the following letter?

Buckskin Bessie

NAVARRE HOTEL
7TH AVE. & 38TH ST.
NEW YORK

Jan. 21, 1913
Navarre Hotel
Times Square Station. N. Y.

Dear Sister,

Arrived in N. York Sat. morning. Leave tomorrow Tues. 21st on the "Kaiser Wilhelm." It will take 7 days. We were down to see our boat; it's a dandy, one of the best ones that float. We are going 1st. class so you can imagine how swell. It will be a little much so to suit me, got to wear evening dresses have your hair dressed and all that sort of stuff but I should worry, I don't pay for any of it so let it be swell. I am taking some cowgirl clothes with me as Mr. Miller is bringing some of his moving pictures and he wants me to fix up in costume and stand around in front of theater. He is going to make spiels on the inside some show. Well I guess this is all will write you again on boat.

The Trip

You write me right away and send
c/o Mr. Billie Burke
303¹/2 Long Acre Building
N. York, N. Y.

The "Kaiser Wilhelm" (picture on chapter page) was a beautiful steamer built in Germany and it made regular trips between New York and Germany. If Bessie was nervous to travel by steamboat after the sinking of the Titanic that had occurred only one year earlier, she does not mention it. Only the prestigious rode in first class.

Extra, Extra:
During 1917 when the war broke out this ship was seized by the U.S. and was then used for the war efforts until, in 1940 when the ship was too old to be used in the Second World War, it was then sold for scrapping.

Many different pictures of Bessie were used on posters and advertisements because of her striking beauty. She preferred her Western clothes and her Western lifestyle but there was not a choice on the ship so she would put up with the fancy clothes and hairdos. This trip was not only a pleasure trip but also a business trip, as Joe spent several weeks arranging for the so-called "big show deal" where they would ship a sizable part of the show in 1913 to perform in Europe. [1]

[1] *The Real Wild West, pg. 398, Michael Wallis*

Buckskin Bessie

NORDDEUTSCHER LLOYD
BREMEN.

D. „KAISER WILHELM II"

Jan. 29, 1913

Dear Sister,

We land in the morning and I am not sorry. I have only been able to be up two days. Never was any more sick. Just laid in bed. I think it was due to the bad weather we had. It was something awful. Could not walk the boat rocked so, I guess this is the worst time of year for travel. Have had some very bad storms. Spose you have see accounts of them in the papers. But the time goes fast it seems only a few days but I much prefer the land.

You can tell some of those high-flown might-ons of yours that I have gone to Europe because they always like to rub it in. That will make them open their eyes.

Guess this is all, will write you tomorrow when we get to Berlin, Germany.

Mr. M. was not much sick but I don't know what would have happen to his mother, she weight over

The Trip

There are several things of interest in this letter. First off, it appears that Mr. Miller's mother, Molly, went along. As you will come to understand, she was vehemently against Joe and Bessie's relationship. That was perfectly understandable, since Joe was married. But even after he was divorced, she would not approve of Bessie. Her dislike of Bessie could have been because she was not a Southern belle like Molly herself who was known as the supreme hostess; whereas, Bessie clearly preferred to ride by Joe's side in parades or on the range. Or she may have simply thought Bessie was a gold digger and taking advantage of her over-the-hill son.

Like so many others, Esther's friends were very critical of Bessie being in a Wild West show, not to mention having an affair. Bessie snagged this opportunity to point out the advantages her choice had given her over them. Most women followed the tradition of marrying a local boy and having lots of babies with no travel in sight and very little money to spend.

Seven days at sea and sick in bed five of them made for a horrid trip, yet she searched for the positive as she always did when she wrote, "the time has gone by quick."

Buckskin Bessie

Hôtel Westminster
Rue de la Paix
Paris

Paris France

Dear Folks,

Got here yesterday. Some city, more English
spoken here so it is much easier to get along. We will leave
Sunday for London. Then I think we will start
home. I've had enough sight seeing, am satisfied to go
back. There is nothing so very wonderful here and we see
it all, ride all over town. The taxies are very reasonable;
you can ride an hour for about 50 cents, big fine cars. At
night we go to all the places that are of importance. We
have met several people we know so it's not hard to get
around, but those swell places sure cost a lot. Some you
cannot get into without spending $25. Can't sit down to a
table some places you can't buy anything but champagne
and they charge $5 a bottle, this is the country where it is
supposed to be cheap. You can get things much cheaper

The Trip

if you go to a smaller place, you pay for the name,
some places you pay $20 for a hat where you can go a
block and get it for $5.

With love,
B.A.H.

This letter begins, "Dear Folks"—but on the envelope, it is addressed to Esther, the same as all the others.

Bessie may be a farm girl/cowgirl, but there is no fooling her. She is quick to figure out things are not all they appear to be in this world of high class and money. But this is a part of Joe's world and one in which he is very comfortable. Perhaps that is one of Joe's greatest strengths. He could be comfortable and equipped in a multitude of settings, in the grandstand and in the fields, in fancy hotels, on a horse, with the Indians, and in any type of business deal. Unquestionably, the reason he had Bessie by his side was she matched his character and was not easily persuaded. The only times that seemed to put Joe on edge were when his mother demanded he leave Bessie behind.

Telegrams: PIQUDILLO, LONDON.
Telephone 160 GERRARD.

PICCADILLY HOTEL

PICCADILLY
& REGENT STREET,
LONDON, **W.**

Piccadilly Hotel
London, England

Dear Folks,
Got here last night, have not seen much of the town

Buckskin Bessie

yet, it is foggy outside, not like our fog, more like smoke. Guess we will stay here until Wed. then we sail for home the 18th Feb. May take a 3 day trip to Ireland from here, it's such a pretty country. Yesterday we were on the water one hour and I sure was sick but the boat was not very large and the sea was rough. I sure dread the boat trip home. I will get some cards and send you. My mail has not been forwarded from N.Y. so I have not had any letter from you, but will when we reach N.Y. I expect.

As Ever, B.A.H.

Extra, Extra:

The hotel Piccadilly is now the luxurious Le Meridien Piccadilly and it is about half the size it was in 1913. Courtesy of Judy Roberts

James Collection —
The building with the three white stacks is the Piccadilly Hotel

The Trip

It would be reasonable to assume that only Bessie had the opportunity to stay in such beautiful hotels due to her "stand in" with Joe, and not the whole group of show people.

1913
Hotel Knickerbocker
New York, N. Y.

Dear Folks,

Just got off the boat, had another stormy trip but not as bad as going over. I was in bed most of the time, just as soon as it gets smooth I'm all right. Was glad to get back again and have a dandy time, but no place like America.

Extra, Extra:

From the online newspaper:

The Morning News
Sept. 9, 2003 | New York, New York

The Knickerbocker lives on. Late last month it emerged from two and a half years under scaffolding, having undergone an estimated $10-million renovation.

It's red-brick, French renaissance façade capped by a copper mansard roof is studded with railings and terra-cotta detailing and yet the most fascinating thing about the Knickerbocker isn't its design, but its history.

When it opened in 1905, the Knickerbocker was one of midtown's premier hotels, and one of the tallest buildings on Times Square. The Knickerbocker boasted 556 rooms, original art by Frederick Remington and Maxfield Parrish, and an immense dining room.

The Knickerbocker even had its own subway entrance, which can still be seen today. It's at the eastern end of Track 1 at the Times Square shuttle platform. (At the time the shuttle was actually part of the IRT tract that ran south along the 4/5/6 line and continued north along the 1/3/9 tracks.) There you'll find a grimy, non-descript door, the lintel of which reads Knickerbocker. The door is locked, but it once gave way to a cozy basement lobby and bar.

Today the hotel is simply called 6 Times Square, and it holds not hotel guests, but an apparel showroom.

"No place like America," as she proudly calls it home.

Chapter 7

Home is Where the Heart is

Bessie holding the head of the foal
James Collection

Buckskin Bessie

Although the show continued from Times Square to Buffalo and then on to Detroit[1] it appears Bessie left the show and made a trip home. The following letter was written on her journey there.

NEW HOTEL SHERMAN
EUROPEAN

March 22, 1913

St. Paul, Minn.

Just got in and that punk Ruthton agent has not got my ticket here, so will haf to stay here tonight and do not know if I will get out tomorrow as he will not be in his office so we can get here by wire but I'll write him a letter that he won't forget for a day or two. I've called this agent everything I could say in English but I guess it is not his fault as he has nothing to do with it yet but I told him he would have to do something so he called all the A. Northern offices but nothing stirring.

B. H.

[1] *The Real Wild West, pg. 400, Michael Wallis*

Home is Where the Heart is

This letter comes four months later:

July 11, 1913

Dear Folks,

Why don't you get busy and write once in a while? I sent Ma some scrim quite a while ago but have not heard if she got it or not. It does not amount to much but I wish someone would write when I send anything so I'll know if it gets there or not. I also sent you some photographs. I have not heard from Dady since I was at your place. I have an Angora cat, gray, sure is cute. Had a letter from Amy a few days ago said maybe her and Roy were going to visit you.

Well, I guess this is all the time I have.

Write,
B.A.H.

Bessie appears to be frustrated and hurt at not hearing from home. She often sent things home and Betty Allen (her niece) recalled, "Every Christmas, we (my sisters and me and my cousins) always received gifts from her. I remember one time along with our gifts she sent a big box of pecans which we really enjoyed. This was during the depression and she seemed to be the only one that had money."

Buckskin Bessie

A scrim was a bolt of fabric.

"Dady" would appear to be misspelled, but in truth she is speaking of Joe. He referred to himself several times as "Dady" in letters written to her[2] and this letter is in 1913 which again reveals that their relationship began several years prior to the 1915 Exposition as was originally thought.[3]

No letters were found through August and September but we can assume she was with the show as they continued their tour through Texas and ended the season in Houston on Oct. 28th. Many of the performers returned to the 101 Ranch where this following letter picks back up.

Nov. 15, 1913
Bliss, Okla.

Dear Sister,

I rec'd your letter. We have been here a couple wks. Have been working for moving pictures about one wk. Will work at that off and on all winter I guess. There are many days when it is cloudy, we don't do anything. Expect to go on a trip sometime but do not know if I will have chance to go home or not, never can tell.

[2] *Jack Keathly interview, Sept 5, 2003*
[3] *The Real Wild West, pg. 428, Michael Wallis*

Home is Where the Heart is

Surely will if I can. Too bad about the boys dying. The boys ought to get busy and skip, before they all die. There are a lot of sick ones here, but just as quick as they get the cholera they ship those that are not sick. Weather is same as summer here. We are the same bunch of girls here and Mr. & Mrs. Rogers. This place is about the same as our (8) is at home, maybe our house is larger. It's a good place to winter; I have my dog and cat. A man on the street car offered our porter $40 for my cat one night. He was bringing her to the car but he was afraid to sell her. I told him it would have been alright and I would have given him $10 of it.

I don't want to write to those girls, it's too much bother. I get letters from lots of people I do not know but never answer. It's a nuisance to write to a lot of people. You can give them post cards.

Write soon,
B. A. H.

Written across the top of the page as if an afterthought was:

Seth's Linsay girl is not here, she told me she was going to write him. I won $40 gold (steer head diamond eyes) from her old man in a horse race a few days before *show closed. He thought he was riding the fastest horse on the show and I had another picked out. Mr. Miller said we had better ride and settle the argument and I won. It's a dandy pin.*

Following is a blown up insert of this pin from the picture found in the scrapbook on page 119. This becomes that other famous steer head with the diamond eyes and close to Bessie's heart.

> **Extra, Extra:**
> Joe Miller's saddle had four of these steer heads, one on each corner of the skirt of his saddle and like Bessie's, they each have diamond eyes but his also include rubies in the nose and other precious stones surrounding the steer head. This cannot be fully appreciated without actually seeing the saddle that is on display at the Woolaroc museum in Bartlesville, OK.[4]

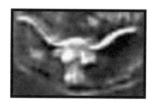

This was a case of "put your pin where your mouth is." She was proud to have won it and this probably was not the only dispute that Joe Miller was to oversee concerning his little spitfire, Bessie.

Esther's friends have now elevated Bessie to a star and want her to write to them; maybe that is why the man offered to buy her cat as well.

[4] *Authors visit to Wooloroc Museum, March of 2005*

Home is Where the Heart is

Nov. 29, 1913
Ponca City, Okla.

Am leaving so don't write here anymore. Will let you know where to write.

Will want you to send some letters.

Expect to be away about 6 wks.

B. H.

This is an unusual letter. She is not saying where she is going or with whom and when she says "Will want you to send some letters," it must be for the purpose of making it appear she is in a particular place as before, rather than for continued correspondence. Six weeks is a long time and even though the 101 show went on tour in South America, leaving November 1, 1913, Bessie was not listed as part of that group or referred to in any available documents such as the Edith Tantlinger diary.[5]

[5] *Edith Tanlinger Diary, University of Oklahoma Library Western History Collection, Norman, Oklahoma*

Buckskin Bessie

Five months later:

Hotel Preston
4th Avenue & 26th St.
(Opp. Mad. Sq. Garden
New York

April 20, 1914
Hotel Preston
New York, N. Y.

Dear Sister,

We arrived about a wk. ago. The show opens in Madison Square Garden the 21st April. Stay here three wks. I saw Bill Dafaoin and his Mother last night.

We sure have some bunch of people. This is all I have time for now, never was so busy before rehearsing all the time. Send mail c/o 101 Ranch Wild West Show

Madison Square Garden

No letters were found from November until this one in April when they are starting the 1914 season. It is possible that Esther chose not to save the letters that contained detailed information and reference to Bessie and Joe being together; adultery/living together

94

was not taken lightly in the year of 1914, but she says "we arrived" so she was not alone.

Just as what she means by, "we have some bunch of people" is not clear. It could mean there are a lot of people, or that many of the people were of questionable character. As well as the famous, the Millers routinely hired outlaws, ex-convicts and, even hardened killers.[6]

Bessie was one of the lead persons in the parade and she was very visible, as she says. But she must have had a lot of other responsibilities as well to be involved with so much rehearsal time. A total of 21 different displays (reenactments and shows) were described in the *101 Ranch* book, along with a rodeo that included roping, trick riding, etc.

Madison Square Garden
James Collection

The show was very popular in Madison Square Garden and they performed there for several weeks at a time. Of special interest were the cowgirls. Unlike the Victorian women, they were tough, wild, and totally natural beauties. The most feminine adornment often being a scarf tied around their neck. In many of the pictures of Bessie, she included a string of white pearls.

[6] *The Real Wild West, pg. 395, Michael Wallis*

Buckskin Bessie

Sept. 3, 1914
Vincennes, Ind.

Dear Sister,

I rec'd a letter from you finally. Am sorry to hear the kittens died but that was better than if Billie would have died.

Tell Mrs. Corey when you write to send it to you and you can forward because the route card would run out before she could write me. How are they getting along? Are they still at Blow Out, Idaho? How come you did not build a bungalow.

I bet Annie is a big girl now. I wanted to have her visit the show this summer, but we never did get near enough. Show has not done as well as usual. Times are so hard but the crops are great wherever we go. I guess the bunch from England will be able to get passage now. They have been holding the boats.

I did not see Judith, wouldn't know her if I did I suppose.

Write soon
B. H.

Home is Where the Heart is

This is Billie, Esther's cat, and she makes reference to her in several of her letters. Since Esther had no children her cat clearly received more attention than most.

The bunch from England she mentions is referring to the group of people that were performing there in August of 1914 when war broke out between Germany and Russia, and the British confiscated and bought all the show horses and wagons for a total of about $80,000 to use in the war effort. This did not begin to reflect the true value of the trained horses and all that was involved. To add to the financial loss, exorbitant funds were required to get all their people safely back to the states. [7]

[7] *The Real Wild West, pg. 424, Michael Wallis*

Feb. 11, 1914
Hotel Paso del Norte
El Paso, Texas,

Dear Sister,

Why don't you ever write? I sent you route card and I know it's run out by now.

Sure is warm here. Well, I'm commencing to think we will go clear to Cal. I am glad we are leaving Texas, do not like this warm country, lots of cotton raised here so there are lots of colored people here.

I am not going to write you much until you write me. How is everything at home? That letter you sent me from Why. I had a hard time to figure out who it was from. I thought it was from a big fat woman we called Mrs. Tie. I met her on the dead Injun hill. Jolly old woman, am going to write to her if I ever get around to it.

Home is Where the Heart is

I am getting much worse than ever before when it comes to writing.

Write quick,
B. A. H.

Again she seems to be longing to hear from home; either Esther was slow to write or Bessie was hard to keep up with. They did end up going all the way to California.

Hotel Paso del Norte

1912

Extra, Extra:
No longer called the Paso del Norte but now the Camino Real. It is listed on the historic hotel registry. It would cost one million to replace the dome if it were done in plastic, much less the original beautiful stained glass.

Whenever it was possible, Bessie would leave the show and make a trip home. The following two letters were during one such trip.

Buckskin Bessie

Nov. 25, 1914
Herman, Minn.

Hello Esther,

    I just got here today and do not know if I will have time to come to Ruthton or not as I am on my way to Frisco, but I want you to come up here while I'm here. Come right away and then if I can go to Ruthton, we can go there together.

    Alma is very anxious for you to come so don't disappoint us.

    B.A. Herberg

Nov, 27, 1914
Herman, Minn.

Dear Sister,

    Yours rec'd I thought you would come. I don't see what would prevent you from coming. I am on my way to Frisco and am quite certain I cannot go to Ruthton because I have to stay here waiting to hear from Frisco. If I should start down there I would be apt to get a message before I get there and besides this is the only address they have so I have my doubts about

Home is Where the Heart is

being able to come to see you. I thought you would like to see the foals anyway.

Etheleen is going with me.

B.A.H.

Bessie's life revolves around the show and the schedules and perhaps she forgets that her sister may have schedules of her own to keep and not be able to come at the drop of a hat, she is clearly disappointed.

> **Extra, Extra:**
> The Wild West show spent 31 weeks on the road during this 1914 season and traveled more than 9,000 by rail. They performed 373 performances at 155 cities in 20 different states.[8]

[8] *The Real Wild West, pg. 418, Michael Wallis*

Below are some of the return addresses on envelopes which contained no letters.

MILLER BROS. & ARLINGTON
101 Ranch Real Wild West
EASTERN OFFICE: RANDALL BUILDING, 136 WEST 52ND STREET
NEW YORK CITY
WESTERN HEADQUARTERS:
BLISS, OKLA.

RETURN IN 5 DAYS TO
BUFFALO BILL (HIMSELF)
AND
101 RANCH SHOWS

GENERAL OFFICE:
1452 BROADWAY, NEW YORK CITY

MILLER BROS. & EDWARD ARLINGTON'S
101 RANCH
REAL
WILD WEST
SHOW
INC.

THE 101 RANCH
WILD WEST SHOW
AFTER 5 DAYS RETURN TO
J. C. MILLER, BLISS, OKLAHOMA.

February 20, 1915 marked the opening of the world's fair in San Francisco, California with the title of The Panama Pacific International Exposition.

Home is Where the Heart is

This beautiful envelope was dated January 1916:

RETURN TO

MILLER BROS.

101 Ranch Real Wild West

PANAMA - PACIFIC EXPOSITION

The Court of Flowers seen on this envelope was only one of the many areas to be experienced. Some of the others were the Court of Four Seasons, the Court of Abundance, the Arch of the Rising Sun, the Palace of Horticulture, the Chinese Pavilion, the Australian Pavilion, the Tower of Progress, the Tower of Jewels, and the Italian Towers. It covered an area of 635 acres but sadly, most of the buildings were made of a temporary plaster-like material and only the Palace of Fine Arts still remains. It was completely reconstructed in 1960.

Extra, Extra:

The Exposition was held in San Francisco to commemorate the celebration of the completion of the Panama Canal and the 400th anniversary of the discovery of the Pacific Ocean by explorer Balboa. The tallest building was The Tower of Jewels at 43 stories high. Not only was it a three-year commitment to construct this worlds fair but also required an expenditure of $50 million dollars. It was reported that a trip to it was equal to a university course as well as the vacation of a lifetime.

This exposition displayed some of the most beautiful sites ever beheld and few that attended would remember that, only nine years before, San Francisco was sitting in the ruins of the earthquake that shook the city and the great devastating fire that followed.

Visitors now beheld beauty at every turn with the array of flowers, lights, exotic foods, the giant scale-model of Yellowstone Park and the Grand Canyon, and a five-acre working replica of the Panama Canal. In the midst of it all was a very popular area called the Zone, an area that was filled with rides, games of skill and chance, performers, and live shows. This was where the 101 Wild West show was located and they dazzled the crowds daily.

Like all the 101 Ranch and Wild West memorabilia, many of the souvenirs from the Expo (such as a watch fob, ribbons, a lucky horseshoe, beautiful serving trays, and the following stamps) are now valuable commodities.

Bessie and Joe

The Parry twins.

Martha Allen
James Collection

Displayed in the 101 Wild West Collection at the Marland's Grand Home Museum located in Ponca City, Oklahoma, is an advertisement for the Miller's newest film of 1915 that was based on an "actual romance that was to have been woven around the Panama-Pacific Exposition."[9] Gracing the front of it is Bessie on her finely attired steed. The consensus of most is that the romance that this was woven around was Bessie and Joe.

This picture is yet another case of mistaken identity. Discovered on a web site, it simply said "Cowgirl Dorothy." When I sent it to Bessie's niece, she said she had never seen it before but it was sure a nice picture of her Aunt Bessie.

[9] *The Real Wild West, pg. 429, Michael Wallis*

Home is Where the Heart is

Jan 8, 1916
Bliss, Okla.

Dear Sister,

Rec'd your letter and the belt. It came just in time as I have got some ribbon to line it with and she never found out I left it behind. We've had some chilly weather too, a couple below zero but that's nothing like you've had. I guess there has been some bad storms around. Our gas all went down so had to burn coal and wood and an oil stove and so many have the gripe, some are awfully sick.

The Colonel has been in bed for several days and had the doctor several times. He was out putting up ice and got wet but guess he will soon be alright.

So Clara has a little girl, rather cold weather to have girls.

How's everything at home? Tell Pet O if I ever get to town will pick out some nice neckties for him but I haven't been to Ponca since I came. It's seven miles and Bliss hasn't anything decent. Tell him I am thinking of getting a Ford. Won't he laugh as I always roasted them. Well, anyway for a rough all around car I think it's the best. I will have it painted a bright

Buckskin Bessie

yellow and have it upholstered nice inside.

Guess this is all

Howdy X's Boomh & all

This letter is two years later than the last one that was dated 1914, but it does not appear that Bessie and Esther have had a break in their relationship but rather things are as usual.

The "Colonel" is Joe. He was given that honorary title in 1915 by Oklahoma Governor Robert Lee Williams.[10] It would seem rather clear that they are together and Bessie is caring for him, but the big question is where they are. Yes, they are in Bliss where the 101 Ranch was, but they would not be in the White House with Mother Miller! Are they staying at what became known as the 50-50 Ranch? Or perhaps they are staying in the house Joe established for his wife Lizzie on the North Fork (a five room white frame house with a front porch).[11]

Chilly weather that is below zero? Trying to stay warm burning coal and wood and cooking on an oil stove? Not exactly luxury but true to her character, Bessie seems to be able to be satisfied with much or satisfied with little. At the end of the letter, she says "Howdy to X's Boomh." Esther and Seth divorced and this would indicate it was prior to this letter. A bright yellow car? She clearly was not trying to hide and in fact wanted them to see her coming!

Although the following is only a partial letter, it is of special interest because only Joe Miller is listed as the director on it. This was due to the falling out the three brothers. George and Zack did not want to go on the road again after the problems they had experienced 1915. However, Joe was determined and brought on Buffalo Bill and the military pageant from the United States War Department for the new 1916 show.

The last show of 1916 was held on November 11, 1916 in Portsmouth, Virginia.[12] Not only was this the last show for the

[10] *The 101 Ranch, pg. 30, 34, 35, Collins and England*
[11] *The Real Wild West, pg. 197, Michael Wallis*
[12] *Ibid pg. 459*

108

season, but it was to be the last time Bessie and Joe would dazzle the crowd riding side by side. It was also the last performance of Buffalo Bill. The country mourned Buffalo Bill's death that occurred only two months later on January 10, 1917, and the 101 Wild West Show closed and would not tour again until Zack Miller went back on the road in 1925 with a show that deviated greatly from the original and took on a variety of circus acts and far-eastern entertainment.

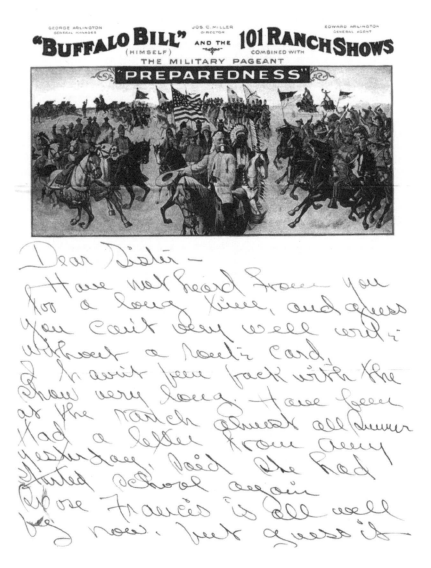

Buckskin Bessie

Feb. 7, 1917
Bliss, Okla.

Dear Sister,

Your two letters rec'd. Have been back a week now. I don't think so much of Florida the land is so punk that is most of it. Every bit of land down there has to be fertilized. You can buy it very cheap from $1.75 to $100 per acre but the cheap land ain't worth a dam. It has to be cleared and then fertilized before you can raise a crop. Then again there are some beautiful orange groves and places just as good as Cal. Sell as high as $500 to 1,000 per acre.

It's a delightful climate; everything is so far behind the times in the country. The large towns are modern and up to snuff same as any larger city but I think I would rather have some land here where I understand the country. We have had no snow to speak of and our winter is about over. No, I don't think I am going to settle down for any length of time but would like to own a place. If I get one would like to have you come and stay a couple months. Think you would enjoy it. Guess Boslick could spare you for awhile.

I hate my Ford, for three days I couldn't make

Home is Where the Heart is

it go, never again do I want a machine that you have to crank, life is too short for that. Am going to try and make a trade and get some kind of Roadster. I'm crazy about them, at least something with a self-starter. You don't know what you are missing by not having a car. There is no fun like driving one, that is all I see is cars. I may go to an automobile school in Kansas City for a couple of months later on. Gasoline is 25 cents a gallon here now but I should worry. I drive just as much.

Well write soon,

As Ever, B

A year between letters and she has now come from Florida. Few today would share Bessie's view of owning land in Florida. Her perspective of owning land, however, was for the purpose of growing crops not for retirees.

Joe spent a lot of time away from the ranch due to his disagreements with his brothers over the show and with his Mother over his relationship with Bessie. His mother was so angry that he would not give up Bessie that she removed him as an heir to her estate. What must it have felt like for Lizzie, Joe's wife, to hear that he refused to give her up even if it meant walking away from his rights, claims, and status as the eldest son of George Miller, the creator of the 101 Empire! Her constant complaint was that he left her alone putting the ranch, the show, and his family over her. She had enough. She packed her bags that spring of 1917 and had her brother draw up divorce papers.[13]

---

[13] *The Real Wild West, pg. 461, Michael Wallis*

Although the door was now open wide for Joe to marry Bessie, that did not happen. Perhaps when we read Bessie's response—"No, I don't think I am going to settle down for any length of time"—it may have indicated that Esther was questioning this illicit relationship between her and Joe.

"If you have to crank it, it isn't worth having." Many people came to this same conclusion. However, she is still crazy enough about cars to want to learn, as she stated many years earlier, and is now thinking she will go to automobile school.

Ten years have come and gone and she is still longing for a place of her own.

Chapter 8

The Scrapbook

Sister Esther and possibly her first husband Seth
James Collection

The Scrapbook

Father, Jonas
James Collection

Daughter, Bessie
James Collection

Buckskin Bessie

MISS BESSIE HERBERG   101 Ranch Cow Girl

A fancy tooled leather saddle but not the one with gold and silver.
Allen Collection

The Scrapbook

Stevens Collection

If you look at her glove upside down you will see the
beaded rider on the bucking bronc.

Buckskin Bessie

Seen with her many pets.
Note: This dress was displayed in the Jack Keathly collection.

Stevens Collection

Notice the steer head pin with the diamond eyes and the string of pearls.
The horseshoe pin surrounds a diamond horse head.

Buckskin Bessie

COW GIRLS, MILLER BROS. 101 RANCH

Parry twins, Bessie and Martha Allen

The Bob White Collection

Bob White Collection

Buckskin Bessie

Miss Bessie Herberg and her educated horse "Happy"
101 Ranch Real Wild West Show.

Bob White Collection

Stevens Collection

A picture almost identical to this one appears in the following book written by Mike Sokoll but in it, he identifies her as Ruth Roach a famous bronc rider, another instance of mistaken identity.

Buckskin Bessie

This friendship between Bessie and Jane Woodend, a famous stage actress, who hiding her true identity, performed in the Wild West Show as a trick rider, should not be a surprise. Both women sacrificed all for their love of the 101.[1]

Bob White Collection

[1] *The Real Wild West, pg. 278, Michael Wallis*

Stevens Collection

Chapter 9

A Place of
Her Own

Bessie
James Collection

Buckskin Bessie

June 18, 1917
Bliss, Okla.

Dear Sister,

Yours rec'd a few days ago. I am all settled now and have a very nice place. Have many chickens and some hogs. Martha's husband is half and half with me on stock. So the boys had to register. I guess they do every place but there is not much chance of them having to go as they do not take any farmers because they need them to raise crops. I suppose if it came to a scarcity of men, it lasted several years, then they would call on them.

No sense worrying until you have to. Had an announcement from Roy, that kid has been going some. I sure am one busy person these days. Have a garden about an acre and on new soil, so you can imagine how the weeds grow.

It seems like Pete Nelson dies young. You ought to come out here for a visit. I guess Billie Cat is trying to populate the world with kittens. I have two registered Airedale pups that I think will make good dogs. They will at least keep the coyotes away. They are bad around here about catching chickens. My wheat is almost *ripe. Will be cut sometime this week. I am going to run the binder for the fellow and it will save him hiring a man only about four days harvesting.*

Guess this is all for now,

Write soon

Am enclosing a few cards of the place. Not very good but we are going to have more taken.

This letter was in an envelope with the return address of:
B.A. Carter
Bliss, Okla.
R _ 2

It comes only four months after the last letter where she says she does not know if she will ever settle down but would like to have land of her own, and it is the first time we now see her use the name of Carter. As was stated earlier, Bessie filled out a 1920 United States census and on the copy of that census that I acquired, she stated she was Bessie Carter and divorced; yet on another copy that was provided to me from a different source, it stated that she was Bessie Carter and a widow. Either way, it can be substantiated that she married a man named Carter by the time of this letter of June 18, 1917, and was either divorced or widowed by 1920. What is not documented is how much time she spent with him, or where. There are accounts that this man named Carter was an Indian and that she married him to give the pretense that she and Joe were no longer lovers, so that Joe would then be in good graces again with his mother and that this marriage to Carter was in name only. It is even possible that there was no marriage at all and that Bessie simply changed her name to give the pretense of marriage. No one really seems to know what this relationship was, but Carter did become her legal name. A point of interest is the fact that she is established here on what has become known as the 50-50 Ranch prior to the death of

Buckskin Bessie

Joe's mother in July 28, 1918. It has always been assumed that the reason for the existence of the 50-50 was simply to take care of Bessie and that it was provided entirely by Joe Miller after he promised to sever his relationship with Bessie on his mother's deathbed.[1] However, these letters and copies of the deeds to the property that will follow show some very different possibilities.

The most obvious things found in this letter are the contentment and peace it reflects. She says, it is "a very nice place." Obviously, fancy was not the criterion of being nice, but rather that she finally has a place of her own. She is not afraid to work, whether it is with Joe or a man named Carter or totally alone.

She refers again to her good friend Martha and that Martha's husband, Clarence Shultz, is an equal partner on the stock with her. Equal partners would usually mean that each person owns fifty percent and neither Joe's name or Carter's name are mentioned as being a part. She is working a small garden, about an acre in size, and she is pulling the weeds by hand! The boys she refers to about registering are most likely both her and Esther's younger brothers. "No sense worrying until you have to," is good advice and probably how she maintained peace in the mist of the whirlwinds that blew through her life.

Isn't it odd that she signs this B.A.H. and not Bessie Carter?

[1] *The Real Wild West*, pg. 466, Michael Wallis

James Collection

Only seven months later, she sent this envelope which was clearly postmarked from a German ship. The date is January 21, 1918 (there was no correspondence inside). This trip most likely was made on the steamship that Joe himself purchased for the cost of $450,000 in 1915. He bought it to transport livestock to Europe in support of the war effort and then later transformed it to accommodate the show's performers.[2] It is questionable if Bessie really went on this trip or simply sent some letters ahead with friends as another decoy because less than three weeks later, the following letter came from Florida.

[2] *Ponca City (Oklahoma) Courier, March 18,1915*

Buckskin Bessie

Feb. 10, 1918
Orlando, Florida

Dear sister,

Yours rec'd. Martha forwarded it to me. I have
been down here for some time, do not know how much
longer we will stay, I sure surprised that Ma is so well
but she had better be careful as it takes a long time after an
operation to heal. Yes, I was at Montgomery, Ala.
When I sent message and went to the Western
Union every day 2 or 3 times for a wk. But there is
(40,000) soldiers there and a good many of them were
sending and getting messages, so it was so crowded you
could hardly get waited on. So in the rush they may have
overlooked mine but I sure did ask for an answer but I
never did get any of your letters only what Martha sent
me. That was nice for Ma that those people looked her
up. Those little nuts are pine nuts, seems she ought to know
them. So Alva had a kidney taken out, well I guess a
kidney more or less won't make much difference to him a little things like that ought not to bother him. It seems opera-
tions are quite the thing in your vicinity. I wrote
Martha to look in my things and see if she can find you
a picture and send it to you. I'm not sure that I have
one left. You ought to be in the chicken business how eggs

132

bring 65 cents per dozen here and chickens 35 cents per pound. That makes a small chicken bring $1.50 a piece. This is one of the prettiest towns in Florida but it's almost to warm to suit me. They wear white suits and panama hats already, guess they do all winter. Okla. Has had more cold and storms than ever before this winter. Guess Ma couldn't hire anyone if she wanted to as help is so scarce, but it's better to pay out money for help than doctor bills. To bad she ain't down in this country you can hire an old nigger woman for $9.00 to 7 dollars per month and they do everything. Women in the South don't think of doing their own work and I don't blame them as it gets so hot you don't feel like doing anything. They would think it awful to be without their nigger servants they bring up the children too and the kids sure like the old mammy. I would want one if I located down here. I like them, they even board themselves. The plantation have several families and they live in little tenant houses and do the farm work, mostly cotton. Tell Seth there will be no little vessels nothing like that in my family, you are more apt to hear of me being single again. Well, I guess this is all for now you can write same address as you did as I don't know where I will be.

Write as ever, B.

Note: The envelope of this letter is postmarked from Jacksonville, Florida. In the letter, she tells Esther to write her at the same address because she does not know where she will be. An odd statement, but the possible answer is the following as quoted from *The Real Wild West*, page 463: "For weeks at a time, Joe traveled far and wide mostly by automobile. He purchased a boatload of range cattle from Honduran ranchers at the stockyards in Jacksonville, Florida."

It continues to talk about the letters he was to have written to Bessie the whole time he was away but perhaps, just like when she first ran off with Joe on the special trip to Europe, they have contrived a way to make it appear that Bessie is there on the ranch and Joe is away. In truth, they are together and the "same address" she speaks of was Martha Allen at the ranch. After Martha received the letters she would then forward them on to where Bessie and Joe were as described in the above letter.

That was quite a breakdown she gave on the worth of a chicken. Surely, she would have been successful at any endeavor she chose.

She is also indicating that she is married and considering getting divorced and that having children didn't seem to be in her future. This would indicate that she and Joe continued their relationship after her name became Carter.

People of today could easily be offended by her remarks of "nigger" but remember times were different in the South in 1918 and this was normal accepted practice.

Extra, Extra:
Arkansas City Traveler, October 19, 1918

"Filming city people, who have been wishing that they could see a real moving picture made, will have the opportunity of doing so tomorrow if they care to drive to Bliss, Oklahoma. Tom Mix and company, which include more than fifty others, have been working on a film playlet called "The Making of a State" at Miller Brothers 101 Ranch; and on Sunday, which is the last day, the ranch will be open to the public from 1:30 to 4:00 p.m."

A Place of Her Own

This took place eight months after the last letter. People from far and wide came to see the making of this movie as well as others that were filmed on the ranch.

As part of my research, I was able to secure six copies of land deeds between Bessie Carter and Joe Miller dated from July 14, 1920 thru May 3, 1923. They were difficult to understand, I consulted a property lawyer and he explained the transactions more clearly. The first deed is record No. 33 and following is a partial copy:

THIS INDENTURE, Made this.....14.................day of..........July.....................A. D. 19.20..,

between.....,..,.:.,.............Bessie A. Carter A Single woman.....................................

of......Noble..........................County, in the State of Oklahoma, of the first part, and..........

...........Bessie A. Carter & J. C. Miller of Bliss, Okla.........................of the second part.

WITNESSETH, That the said part..ies.of the first part, in consideration of the sum of..............

----One & --no/100----.-.-.-.-.-.-.-.-.-.-.-.-.-.-.-.-.-.-and.-.-.-.-.-.-.DOLLARS,

the receipt whereof is hereby acknowledged, do........by these presents grant, bargain, sell and convey unto said parties......of the

second part,.....their.....heirs and assigns, all of the following described REAL ESTATE, situated in the County of Noble, and

State of Oklahoma, to-wit:.t-eat-Half--of--the-North-west--quarter-af-section--Twenty-Seven--(27)....
and the North west quarter of the Northeast quarter of section Twenty-Eight (28)
all in Township Twenty Four (24) North of Range Two(2) East of the Indian Meridian,
containing 120 acres more or less.

TO HAVE AND TO HOLD THE SAME, Together with all and singular the tenements, hereditaments and appurtenances thereunto belonging or in any wise appertaining forever.

And said .....Bessie A. Carter a single woman.

for...her..........heirs, executors or administrators, do......hereby covenant, promise and agree to and with said part..y...of

second part, that at the delivery of these presents.she.is.......lawfully seized in....her........own right of an absolute and indefeasible estate of inheritance, in fee simple, of and in all and singular the above granted and described premises, with the appurtenances; that the same are free, clear, discharged and unincumbered of and from all former and other grants, titles, charges, estates, judg-

ments, taxes, assessments, incumbrances of what nature or kind soever;.................and other......................
Except a certain mortgage to Central State Bank of Ponca City, for Twenty Seven
Hundred Dollars which second parties assume and agree to pay
and that they she

will warrant and forever defend the same unto said part...y...of the second part, ...their.......heirs and assigns, against said

part..ies.of the first part.....their.....heirs, and all and every person or persons, whomsoever lawfully claiming or to claim the same.

This is a small piece of property that Bessie Carter owned solely as a single woman. It had a mortgage of $2,700 to Central State

Bank. She is now transferring it to Bessie Carter & J.C. Miller. The title cannot be sold or transferred unless they both sign; meaning they each owned an undivided one-half interest. As noted by the attorney I consulted, "It was highly unusual for a single woman to be able to secure a loan and own property in this period of time."

Because there are letters written from Bessie on 50-50 Ranch stationery prior to the date of this deed (on pg.135), it is clear that she owned or managed the 50-50 Ranch before she transferred this property into her and Joe's names. Which indicates that this could be the 50-50 and she acquired it while married and widowed or divorced from Carter.

Extra, Extra:
It's important to know that in order for an Indian to sell his land, he first had to be declared competent by the Indian Department in Washington. Proof of competency, however, was not required to lease their land.

THIS INDENTURE, Made this 14 .... day of .... July .... A. D. 19 20 .,
between .... J.H. Ledbetter & Belle Ledbetter, his wife ....

....

of .... Noble .... County, in the State of Oklahoma, of the first part, and ....

.... Bessie A. Carter & J.C. Miller .... of the second part.

WITNESSETH, That the said part Y .... of the first part, in consideration of the sum of ....

.... One & no/100 .... and .... DOLLARS,

the receipt whereof is hereby acknowledged, do .... es .. by these presents grant, bargain, sell and convey unto said part ies .... of the

second part, .. their .... heirs and assigns, all of the following described REAL ESTATE, situated in the County of Noble, and

State of Oklahoma, to-wit: ....

South Half of the North East Quarter of Section Twenty eight, Township
Twenty four Range 2 East of Indian Meridian, Noble County, Okla. containing
eighty acres more or less.

The second deed of record which was recorded on the exact same date as the first one follows:

Again we see that it cannot be sold or altered unless both agree. This property was already in Joe's name according to the land description given for the Deed of Trust that was formed between the brothers in 1921[3] and undoubtedly his prized apple orchard that his Mother left him[10] (when Joe's mother removed him from her will, she had a change of heart and allowed him to keep this apple orchard).

It would appear they are joining their separate properties to become one together. The Ledbetter's probably were only a conduit to make the transfer.

This next document was dated September 10, 1921:

OIL AND GAS MINING LEASE

AGREEMENT, Made this......10'.....day of.....September.............192..1. by and between.......Bessie A. Carter a Single person and J.C. Miller a Single man person

of........Bliss, Oklahoma........................... and ....Gypsy Oil Company, a corporation

hereinafter respectively called lessor and lessee, whether one or more.

That the lessor, for and in consideration of the sum of.....................One and no/100 - - - - - .... DOLLARS,

paid by lessee, receipt of which is hereby acknowledged, and of the covenants and agreements hereinafter contained on the part of the lessee to be kept and performed, has granted, demised, leased and let, and by these presents does grant, demise, lease and let unto the lessee, for the sole and only purpose of mining and operating for oil and gas, installing gas pumps, laying pipe lines, building tanks, stations and structures thereon to produce, store and convey said products, all that certain tract of land situated in the county of NOBLE, STATE OF OKLAHOMA, described as follows, to-wit: The west-half of the North-west Quarter (W ½] of section Twenty-Seven (27) Township Twenty Four North (24N) Range two East (2E) AND, The South half of the North-East Quarter (S½ N½] of section Twenty Eight (28) Township Twenty Four North (24N) Range Two East (2E)

of Section...27 & 28 Township.....24N..........., Range. R= .28............... containing.../..........One Hundred Sixty (160)........acres more or less.

TO HAVE AND TO HOLD the same for a term of five years from this date and as long thereafter as oil or gas or either of them is produced from said land by lessee, ...its.............successors, or assigns.

In consideration of the premises, the lessee covenants and agrees:
FIRST: To pay the lessor as royalty one-eighth part of the proceeds of all the oil saved and sold from that produced on said premises and to run such oil to pipe line companies to which lessee may connect.....its..........well or wells under division orders placing one-eighth part of said proceeds to lessor's credit, or at lessee's option, to pay the lessor one-eighth part of the market value of such oil in the field where produced on the day the same is sold, run or stored, and in this last event, settlement shall be made by lessee by the 15th day of each month for the royalty accrued during the preceding month.

It is also titled (Bessie A. Carter and J.C. Miller) and covers the property listed previously that they already owned together but now is giving an oil and gas lease concerning it.

---

[3] *The 101 Ranch, pg. 233, Collins and England*

Buckskin Bessie

Stevens Collection

The next recorded deed is dated, July 14, 1922, and shows that Bessie A. Carter is now selling a totally different parcel (for one dollar) of 40 acres that was in her name only to now become titled, Bessie A. Carter and Joseph C. Miller. There is no clue as to how she owned this land that she is now transferring into her and Joe's name. Was Bessie somehow a part of the illegal transfer of Indian property that became the controversy that surrounded the Millers and ushered them into a federal trial in 1923?[4]

---

[4] *The Real Wild West, pg. 476, Michael Wallis*

A Place of Her Own

A partial copy follows:

Given under my hand xxx in the District of Columbia the Sixteenth day of June in the year of our Lord
One Thousand Nine Hundred and Twenty two and of the Independence of the United States the One Hundred and
forty Sixth.

 (G.L.O. Seal) By the President Warren O.Harding

           By Viola B.Pugh Secretary

     M.P.LeRoy Recorder of the General Land Office .

  Recorded;Patent Number 868048

Filed for record on this 14 day of July 1922 at 11.40 A.M.

      (seal) Mrs S.A.Moore County Clerk

       WARRANTY DEED.

       KNOW ALL MEN BY THESE PRESENTS?

That Bessie A.Carter a single person of Noble County,State of Oklahoma, party of the first part, in consideration
of the sum of One Dollar and other valuable considerations,Dollars in hand paid, the receipt of which is hereby
acknowledged, do hereby grant, bargain, sell and convey unto Bessie A.Carter and Joseph O.Miller of Kay County,
State of Oklahoma, parties of the second part, the following described real property and premises situated in
Noble County, State of Oklahoma, to-wit;

     Northwest Quarter of the Northeast Quarter of section Twenty -eight Township Twenty Four North
of Range two East of the I.M. containing 40 acres ,more or less. Together with all improvements thereon and the
appurtenances thereunto belonging and warrant the title to the same.

To have and to Hold said described premises unto the said parties of the second part, heirs and assigns forever,
free, clear and discharged of and from all former grants, charges, taxes and judgements mortgages and other
liens and encumbrances of whatsoever nature.

      Signed and delivered this 10th day of July 1922

Buckskin Bessie

James Collection

Below is a copy of the original picture that was used for the custom made stationery from the 50-50 Ranch.

Stevens Collection

B. A. Carter

This is a partial letter (the first part of it is missing) with no date.

50-50 Ranch

STOCK RAISING AND FARMING

Bliss, Oklahoma

Spose you have planted some garden by now. I had a letter from Annie, she graduates in a month. I sent her $15.00. Was all I could afford, would have like to have bought her some white slippers too. How are the boys coming with their spring work, guess they have most of it done. Have you all of Billier kittens yet? Did Pa get the tobacco I sent him from St. Paul? Don't be so scared to write a little, at least a dozen words.

As Ever, B

Her reference to the kittens of Esther's cat reveals that this letter is still to Esther. Times must be a little hard now since she says she cannot afford to give the slippers, too. She never forgets the spring planting, the storms, the harvesting and etc. Why does she say not to be scared to write? Is she teasing or is there a reason behind it?

Interestingly, the next deed of record (no. 38) to follow reveals that Bessie A Carter, a single woman on April 30, 1923, sells all her rights of all the above-listed properties to J. C. Miller for one dollar and that there is now a mortgage on the property held by the Federal Land Bank of Wichita, Kansas, in the amount of $6,500.

Buckskin Bessie

My legal consultant said, "You probably would find that Joe Miller borrowed money on that property around May 1, 1923, and the bank would only loan it to him if it was in his name only." That casual prediction became an overwhelming possibility when I was able to document that Joe Miller and his two brothers were facing an upcoming federal trial in 1923 for illegally acquiring Indian land. They shocked everyone by pleading guilty and paying a $10,000 fine, even though they had assembled a large, expensive defense team. By far, this was not the first brush the Millers had with the law. In fact, Joe Miller was already a convicted felon who had done time in prison in 1897 for passing counterfeit money.[5]

Deed of record, no. 38 follows:

THIS INDENTURE, Made this......30......................................day of......April..A. D. 192.3...

between ....Bessie.A.Carter.single..

of............Noble........................County, in the State of Oklahoma, of the first part, and.......................................

...........................J.C.Miller.single.of.Marland,Okla...of the second part.

WITNESSETH, That the said party........of the first part, in consideration of the sum of.......................................

.........-One.and..No/100.-.-.-.-.-.-.-.-.-.-.-.-.-.-and.-.-.-.-.-.-.-.-.-.- DOLLARS,

the receipt whereof is hereby acknowledged, do..es..by these presents grant, bargain, sell and convey unto said part..y.......

of the second part,..his..................heirs and assigns, all of the following described REAL ESTATE, situated in the County

of Noble, and State of Oklahoma, to-wit:...

     An Undivided One-half interest in and to the NE¼ of Sec Twenty-Eight(28) and the West ¼ of the NW¼ of Sec. Twenty-Seven (27)s Township Twenty Four (24) North,Range Two (2) East, of the Indian Meridian, according to the Government Survey thereof.

     TO HAVE AND TO HOLD THE SAME, Together with all and singular the tenements, hereditaments and appurtenances thereunto belonging or in any wise appertaining forever.

     And said ....Bessie.A.Carter,.single......for.herself.and.her...

forx..................heirs, executors or administrators, do..es.hereby covenant, promise and agree to and with said party.......

of second part, that at the delivery of these presents..they........lawfully seized in......their........own right of an absolute and indefeasible estate of inheritance, in fee simple, of and in all and singular the above granted and described premises, with the appurtenances; that the same are free, clear, discharged and unincumbered of and from all former and other grants,

titles, charges, estates, judgments, taxes, assessments, incumbrances of what nature or kind soever;.......................

Subject,however to a certain mortgage to the Federal Land Bank of Wichita,Kansas and in 'amount of $6500.00

.....and.that.they...she................will warrant and forever defend the same unto said part..y........of the second part,

.....her..........heirs and assigns, against said part..y.....of the first part...his......heirs, and all and every person or persons, whomsoever lawfully claiming or to claim the same.

     IN WITNESS WHEREOF, the said part..y........of the first part ha..s......hereunto set..her..hand................the day and year first above written.

...........Bessie-A.Carter..............

[5] *Ponca City (Oklahoma Territory) Courier, March 11, 1897*

A Place of Her Own

This is the last recorded deed between Bessie and Joe and it is dated May 3, 1923:

THIS INDENTURE, Made this......3rd..............................day of............May.......................A. D. 19?5.....

between .........J.C.Miller,..a..single..man,...

of...............Kay.......................County, in the State of Oklahoma, of the first part, and...

...........................Bessie..A.Carter..party.................of the second part.

WITNESSETH, That the said party.........of the first part, in consideration of the sum of...............................

.................................*............and.. DOLLARS,

the receipt whereof is hereby acknowledged, do...........by these presents grant, bargain, sell and convey unto said part.......y......

of the second part,...........her...........heirs and assigns, all of the following described REAL ESTATE, situated in the County

of Noble, and State of Oklahoma, to-wit :..

An Undivided one-half interest in and to the Northeast Quarter of section Twenty-eight
(28); West Half of Northwest Quarter of section Twenty-Seven(27) Township Twenty Four
(24) North, Range Two(2) East of the Indian Meridian, containing 240 acres of land,
more or less. according to the Government survey thereof.

TO HAVE AND TO HOLD THE SAME, Together with all and singular the tenements, hereditaments and appurtenances thereunto belonging or in any wise appertaining forever.

And said ....Grantors...for..himself..and..his...................................

for....................heirs, executors or administrators, do..as.hereby covenant, promise and agree to and with said part......y......

of second part, that at the delivery of these presents he..is..........lawfully seized in..........his..........own right of an absolute and indefeasible estate of inheritance, in fee simple, of and in all and singular the above granted and described premises, with the appurtenances; that the same are free, clear, discharged and unincumbered of and from all former and other grants,

titles, charges, estates, judgments, taxes, assessments, incumbrances of what nature or kind soever;..................xxxxxx that Except a mortgage for $6500.00 to the Federal Land Bank,recorded in Book _____ at page.x_____ in the office of the County Clerk of Noble County,Oklahoma.The grantor herein reserves unto himself,his heirs or assigns, an undivided ½ interest in and to all oil,gas and other minerals in xxx or under said lands,
..and..that..he..........................will warrant and forever defend the same unto said part......y.........of the second part,

.........he..........heirs and assigns, against said part.y.......of the first part her...........heirs, and all and every person or persons, whomsoever lawfully claiming or to claim the same.

IN WITNESS WHEREOF, the said part.y...........of the first part has..........hereunto set..his..hand...*.*.*.*.*.the day and year first above written.

..........................J.C.Miller...

Warranty Deed....

What this essentially says is that J.C. Miller now titles all the above previous property back into his and Bessie A. Carter's name (with the same mortgage of $6,500) but with the exception that he now solely keeps all the oil and gas rights. There are no other documents showing this property being sold or transferred.

Buckskin Bessie

Another partial letter with no date.

Hello Cheet,

Got the letters you sent me O.K. No I did not stay long in St. Paul and no telling when I will get back up that way. Waid has not gone yet, but expect to the 28th of this month. Will, his brother was called but they give him a little longer time on account of his wife going to be confined. Well, it looks as though there would be no fight in St. Paul or any other place. Guess the boys will be some disappointed. It's sure too bad, as I would have had you dandy seats ringside that other people pay $25.00 a piece for. We have had two days of awful————

She has never addressed a letter to "Cheet" before this one, so it is not clear who this was.

As men were being drafted at that time, that is no doubt what she is referring to when she writes about Waid and his brother Will. "Will's wife is going to be confined," leaves a lot to our imagination. It could mean a hospital or jail or something entirely different.

The fight she is speaking of is one of the Jess Willard fights. Willard was a boxer known as the "Great White Hope." He joined the Wild West show around 1915[6] and fought six times and had many exhibitions with the 101 Ranch in 1916.

[6] *The Real Wild West*, pg. 431, Michael Wallis

A Place of Her Own

This is another partial letter on this same 50-50 Ranch stationery, and is most likely written to Esther. It appears to be the second page of a letter.

Saying Mrs. Jonas Herberg was a patient there and her condition was very good and she was doing nicely, but they always say that about their patients, so that didn't tell me any thing. Then I sent Seth a message but no response from him. Now I wish you would write and tell me how Ma is and everything. Will send this to Ruthton, but guess it will be sent on to you. I also sent one to Ma for you thinking that if you were with her, you would surely get one.

Signed:

Buckskin Bessie

The most shocking part of this letter is that she has signed it:

Mrs. J. W. Lessert

Bliss, Okla.

c/o Clarence Schultz

R-2

However, it documents conclusively that she was the owner /manager of the 50-50 prior to her mother's death in April of 1918, the same year Joe's Miller's mother died and before the first land deed between her and Joe dated 1920.

No one I was able to locate had ever heard of this name Lessert, and there were no legal documents that showed this becoming her legal name. Why she signed this letter this way is a mystery. Did she did indeed marry a J.W. Lessert? Or is it yet another decoy? The address of R-2 was the same address as on the previous envelope that was from B.A. Carter. I was able to locate a small amount of information about a J.W. Lessert on a United States census which showed a large family living there during this time period. Indeed, there was a son with this name. He was half Indian. But he was a young child at the time of this letter and would have been too young to be married. No one has ever heard of this marriage—not her family, not other historians, no one. But here it is in her handwriting: Mrs. J.W. Lessert.

Our minds swim with questions. Sadly, however, it is just the beginning of the silent years that lie ahead.

Chapter 10

The Silent Years

James Collection

Buckskin Bessie

A 23-year gap lies between the previously written letters and the last one in the following chapter. What happened during all this time? It is unlikely that she and Esther did not maintain their relationship and the picture below documents that; yet, there were no letters saved in the packet throughout this time.

Bessie and Esther
James Collection

Easily revealed was the fact that Bessie was with Joe a good part of the time and was on the move, perhaps using different names. Esther, too, may have been on the move with her divorce and getting remarried. So maybe the letters were simply lost or accidentally thrown out. Or perhaps Betty Hislop Fillion (Bessie's niece where these letters were found in the estate sale) chose to take the missing letters with her, leaving behind when she moved the ones I discovered. It is even possible that someone else bought the missing letters from the estate sale and they are holding another piece of the puzzle. Even without all the letters, we know through research some things that took place during this otherwise silent span.

Bessie's mother, Berta (Britta) Herberg, passed away on April 11, 1918. She is buried in Ruthton, Minnesota.

Joe promised his mother on her deathbed that he would sever his relationship with Bessie.[1]

Joe Miller's mother, Molly Miller, passed away on July 28, 1918. She is buried in the I.O.O.F. Cemetery in Ponca City, Oklahoma, alongside her husband. Strangely, Bessie and Joe both lost their mothers within three months of each other.

The 101 Wild West Show closed for good in 1918 with substantial losses, even with selling off all the equipment.[2]

January 16, 1920 was the beginning of prohibition. A law, that was in effect for 13 years and brought the opposite results of its intended purpose.

In 1920, the 19th Amendment was passed which gave women the right to vote.

Bliss, Oklahoma, became Marland, Oklahoma in 1922, in honor of the oil tycoon, E.W. Marland.

Perhaps because the self-contained city of the 101 seemed able to withstand the effects of things like the prohibition of 1920, it was lulled into thinking everything was fine. But everything was not fine; not on the home front nor in the world. In fact, turmoil abounded with the Great Depression, the fall of the stock market, and the Oklahoma dust bowl which created a huge migration of people from Oklahoma to California and thus creating that famous story *The Grapes of Wrath*.

The Model A Ford was created in 1927 and Amelia Earhart became the first woman to fly solo over the Atlantic. While these are only a few highlights of the many historical events that occurred over this large span of time, we are without a clue as to what Bessie's personal life was like. The one thing we do know is that she survived, and survival may have been her best effort.

---

[1] *The Real Wild West, pg. 466, Michael Wallis*
[2] *Ibid. pg. 462*

Buckskin Bessie

What were her thoughts as her life as a Wild West performer, a life that had consumed her for over seven years, suddenly came to an end? The thrill of the audiences applause, the travel, all quieted, and with them the security of a steady income and many of her friends and associates leaving and her decision to stay behind with Joe. Were there promises made?

What really happened between her and Joe? When did they part ways? Did they part on friendly terms or was it a bitter ending? When did she leave the 50-50 Ranch? Did she remarry while yet on the ranch only to later buy the little store at White Eagle in 1934?

What did it feel like to see the show go on the road again in 1925 and not be part of it? Maybe people accepted an older, fatter Zack perched on Joe Miller's jewel-studded saddle as the lead man in the parade, but only the young and beautiful would ride by his side.

It can only be imagined what it must have been like for her when Joe married a young girl in 1926 who often was mistaken for being his daughter, and then delivered him a son exactly nine months later[3] which deemed him to be a new father and a grandfather at the same time. A son who was first named by his mother and then had his name changed by his father to Will Brooks Miller in honor of Joe's favorite cousin.[4] Yes, the same cousin seen in the picture with Bessie on page 65.

Or imagine the heartbreak watching her very own friends, the Osage Indians, when they gave Joe and his new young bride a wedding celebration that was as large as any of the Wild West shows ever staged at the ranch. A tribal ritual that was reserved for only those with the greatest esteem amongst the Osage tribe and maybe one that Bessie dreamt of sharing with Joe Miller, the love of her life. Instead, here he was with this young bride who knew nothing of Ranch life, nothing of the 101 show, and nothing of the Indians that were bestowing this great honor on her, and really nothing about the man who stood at her side. In fact, she left the 101 with the baby shortly after Joe's funeral never to return.[5]

Perhaps the most shocking of all was the news of Joe's death in

---

[3] *The Real Wild West,* pg. 500, Michael Wallis
[4] *Ibid.* pg. 501
[5] *Ibid.* pg. 504

1927, only one year after the marriage that was the talk of the town. The man she had spent nearly 15 years with. Where was she when she got the news? What were her thoughts about the circumstances surrounding his death? Joe's untimely death was ruled "accidental carbon monoxide poisoning."[6] Can you not help but wonder why there were not more questions and suspicions about such a thing? It had also been speculated that he had suffered a heart attack just before and was the reason he fell unconscious and was not able to escape the deadly fumes. Doesn't it seem that the possibility of foul play would have been more in question? What about the fact that Joe had just told two employees to pack their things and leave the ranch and never come back because of a fight that had broken out between them?[7] Or that his brother Zack was the last one to see him alive and knew he was going to work on the car and upon each of the brother's death a large sum of insurance would go to the surviving brothers? Not to mention the possibility that someone the Millers crossed in the past may have decided to get even. It was no secret that the Millers had crossed the lines of the law more than once. Were there suspicions that could have surrounded Bessie herself, who could have been considered a jilted lover? If any of those things were considered, they were not to be substantiated in accounts of the death of Joe Miller on October 21, 1927.

Did Bessie attend Joe's funeral held six days after his death? Hundreds attended the funeral which was held on the lawn of the "White House"—people from all walks of life, coming to pay their last respects. Was she part of the crowd somewhere? Even Joe's favored stallion was present and took part in the elaborate ceremony,[7] perhaps the very horse that he rode along Bessie's side. She probably knew personally many of the people who were there, especially all of the Ponca Indians. But true to all of her life with Joe Miller, there was no proper place for her.

What went wrong? Joe and Bessie were soul mates. Most people would have agreed to that, with the obvious exception of Joe's Mother. Did Joe really keep his promise to his mother to sever the

[6] *The Real Wild West, pg. 502, Michael Wallis*
[7] *Ibid, pg. 504*

relationship as some have implied? Or did Bessie just lose her attractiveness to Joe? Perhaps he went out and kicked up his heels one night and got caught and was then forced into making things right. Or maybe Bessie finally gave up her hopes of having any real future with Joe and decided she needed to establish a life on her own. There are plenty of questions, but very few answers.

Bessie may have become famous as a 101 Wild West performer and Joe Miller's lover; however, those were just the results of some of the decisions she made in her life, not because of who she was. Her letters have given us little glimpses into the unique woman she truly was. Joe Miller could and often did have any woman he wanted. Yet it was Bessie that he held onto for nearly 15 years. I am sure there are many reasons they were so tightly bound, but some obvious things they had in common were:

Their mutual love of the land. Joe Miller was the reason for the 101 Ranch's tremendous success in the agricultural business. And in Bessie's letters, we see time and time again her making note of the land and always being drawn to it. In the Jack Keathly collection, there was a picture of Joe standing in a beautiful arbor of roses. After comparing the pictures I had brought of the 50–50 Ranch, it was clear that it too had been taken there on the ranch they shared.[8] It struck me that in the very first letter of 1907, Bessie talked about her roses at home and here she was still tending roses more than 20 years later.

Grand entrances. Bessie was one of the lead riders in the parade, a position with which she was very comfortable. I have no doubt that is why she also wanted a brightly yellow painted car. Joe was a showman through and through and even though he loved the land, he loved the applause more, even continuing to the point of jeopardizing the ranch itself. The 1916 Wild West show began with a successful start but soon experienced dwindling audiences and profits due to the death of Iron Tail, the famous Indian on the buffalo nickel, the pressure of the political persuasions against the display of the Military pageant that was then part of the show and the epidemic of polio that struck the nation's children. Even Joe was struck with

---

[8] *Interview with Jack Keathly, Ponca City, Okla. Sept. 5, 2004*

influenza and had to be hospitalized but he insisted the show go on and the Ranch was forced to make up the financial difference jeopardizing the home front and infuriating his brothers.

An interest in language. She studied shorthand and he learned the Indian Siouan language as well as Indian sign language.

Traveling. They traveled for weeks at a time, even when not in the show, and never seemed to tire of it.

Lifestyle. Lastly, they both were very comfortable with the Indian people and often seemed to prefer their company over others. Perhaps that was due because of the simplicity found in the Indian way of life, their honor of the land, and their loyalty.

You cannot spend nearly 15 years with someone and there not be a strong bond built between the two of you. While often those bonds include family and children, such was not the case with Bessie and Joe. Their bonds were their aloofness, their understanding and acceptance of separation, the secrets that only they shared, and the memory of it all.

Turmoil continued on the home front with the death of George Miller occurring only 16 months after that of his older brother Joe.

The Oklahoma Almanac, **1930**
"George Miller, 49, one of the owners of the famous 101 Ranch was wedged under his automobile which skidded on slippery pavement about half way between Ponca City and the Ranch. His skull was crushed and he died before reaching the hospi-

---

She even saw that enormous empire, the 101 Ranch come tumbling down. After struggling for years to overcome their enormous financial problems, Zack sold the livestock and equipment in 1932. Even the household furnishings of the White House were sold off in the end.[9] How inconceivable this must have seemed. The Millers had always had the power and influence and ruled their land and business with an iron hand. Now it was all collapsing like a house of

[9] *The Real Wild West, pg. 515, Michael Wallis*

cards. It is possible that Bessie may have watched all these events from the porch of the 50-50 fully aware that her past, present, and future were disappearing right before her eyes.

In the late 1920s or early 1930s, Bessie married again. She was now Bessie Blackwell,[10] but it was a union not of bliss. She eventually left the 50-50 and in 1934, moved to White Eagle, Oklahoma. What now are her joys? Her friends will tell you that it was her animals, her flowers and her land where she often went out and sat under the big tree.

[10] *The Real Wild West, pg. 466, Michael Wallis*

Chapter 11

One More Parade

James Collection

Buckskin Bessie

The Last letter

Oct. 13, 1941

Bessie Blackwell
RR4
Ponca City, Okla.

Dear Sister,

Rec'd your letter & will ans. now. Just wrote to Little Bit, she is all enthused about the pheasant season opens the 15th Oct. but I don't think I'll go there be more apt to come your way. Say how can a person reach you by (phone). Let me know so Fred can call you if he goes out there to look you up as he doesn't stay very long when goes to Los A. See if you can find a Joe Richesen in the telephone book in Las. A. He used to be with the 101 show and we left him there. I heard he was in the real estate business. There is a lady here from Oakland, Calif. visiting her daughter and she says my flowers are just as pretty as those they have there. We have had a good wet season.

Well, I guess it's about mail time. I am enclosing you a picture of the parade. It's awfully small,

One More Parade

good of my horse but I had my head turned.

B. B.

Written on the back: September 15, 1941
James Collection

September 15th was Bessie's birthday and what a splendid way to spend it but to ride in a parade on her beloved sorrel saddle horse with the exquisite saddle given to her by Joe Miller.[1] This saddle was to have matched Joe's in value and his contained 166 diamonds, 120 sapphires, 17 rubies and 15 pounds of gold and silver.[2]

[1] *The Real Wild West, pg. 466, Michael Wallis*
[2] *Woolarac Collection*

Extra, Extra:

Chronicles of Oklahoma
Volume 19, No. 4
December, 1941

"September 1893 was re-lived in the minds of hundreds of Pioneers and before the eyes of thousands of younger spectators when Ponca City celebrated the 48th anniversary of the Cherokee Strip on September 15th. On the official day of the celebration a pioneer parade passed down the length of Ponca City's main street from 10 o'clock until 11:30.
(Note: This parade continues yet today every September.)

It is only suiting that in this last letter that we have, she is talking about her flowers, a parade, and her horse. These are things she held dear. The letter was addressed to E. M. Patwell, in Hollywood, California. Esther is now remarried and living there.

Little Bit was a nickname for her niece, Betty Hislop. Below is a picture of a pin that was included in the packet of letters with "Little Bit" written on the front of the paper and on the back "Made by Sioux Indian."

According to my interview with Maynard Hislop (Betty Hislop's brother and Bessie's nephew) the estate sale where these letters were discovered and purchased was that of his sister Betty Hislop Fillion. She supposedly decided to move to California, but Maynard said that he'd "not heard from her or been able to contact her." So her whereabouts are unknown. He went on to share that his sister Betty and their Aunt Esther lived together in Hollywood for many years and that is probably why Betty had these letters in her possession. The question remains, however, why she would save them all these years and then leave them behind? Later, there will be some copies of letters that were written to this niece, Betty Hislop, concerning the death of her Aunt Bessie.

In this last letter, we see her sign it Bessie Blackwell. Not much is known about Bessie's last husband, Marshall Blackwell, but following is a copy of his obituary found in the Ponca City News on August 4, 1971. He and Bessie owned two small stores in Oklahoma, one in White Eagle just outside of Ponca City and the other Ardmore. These towns are about 200 miles apart. Bessie ran the store there in White Eagle and Marshall ran the other one while they were married. I question the accuracy of them owning both the stores due to the probate of her estate (following) and also because according this article, Marshall stayed at the store at White Eagle and ran it after Bessie's death until around 1968. It does not appear he ever went back to Ardmore. So it is more likely that he just managed a store at Ardmore.

Death Claims Former Grocer At White Eagle

AUG 4 1971

Marshal M. Blackwell, former longtime grocer at White Eagle, died Tuesday in the Veterans Hospital at Muskogee after a long illness. He was 76.

Burial rites will be in Odd Fellows Cemetery here at 2 p.m. Thursday following services at 10 a.m. in Vinita. Burckhalter Funeral Home of Vinita has charge of arrangements.

A World War I veteran of the Medical Corps, Blackwell had been active in the American Legion. He was born Feb. 24, 1895, at Vinita, which had been his legal residence for about the past two years.

Blackwell owned and operated the Blackwell Grocery at White Eagle for many year, ill health forcing him to give it up about three or four years ago.

His only survivor is a sister, Mrs. Goldie Alumbaugh of Vinita.

Courtesy of Librarian, Kimberlee Yeakley

Buckskin Bessie

Strangely, the people I interviewed in Ponca City did not seem to have any knowledge of Marshall Blackwell, yet here it states that he was part of this community for many years. He was ten years younger than Bessie and it was reported that he was friends with Al Capone. This is not just a far-fetched idea, as Al Capone attempted to purchase the 101 Ranch to convert it into a colony for the Italian families in 1929.[3]

Referencing the letter—it is not known who Fred is or why he would be traveling from Ponca City to California.

Included in the packet of letters were a few written from other family members to Esther, and below are some excerpts from one such letter that was written by Alma (Bessie's and Esther's older sister).

Herman, Minn.
Nov. 12, 1930

I enjoyed my trip to Okla. It's the most of any-thing I ever done, But did not enjoy my visit with Betty. I hate to say so but she don't treat anyone decent. Fred and I did not stay there long. We stayed with the boys most of the time.

Pete and Art and family's are certainly nice to everybody but they and Etheleen went home sooner then they had planned. I liked her man he made us feel wel-come. Her place is not so nice now. It is so run down. Betty is hard up and it was so dry when we were there. It did not look nice but I suppose it would in the spring when things are fresh.

[3] *The 101 Ranch, back cover, Collins and England*

Remember that Bessie's family called her Betty, not Bessie. Had Bessie become bitter and hard to get along with? Or was she on edge because of problems already arising between her and Marshall? It could also have been just an older sister agitation; but whatever it was, Alma was not at all happy with the situation. It can be assumed that "her man" was Marshall Blackwell since they were to have married in the late twenties or early thirties and according to Alma the place was not as nice as it had been and Bessie is hard up now. That seemed to be an odd statement since she implied she had never gone there before. Perhaps she is going by pictures she had seen of the place. If so, then the place was most likely the 50-50 and Marshall and Bessie were newly married. Following are some pictures believed to have been taken during this visit. Etheleen and Amy are two of Bessie's nieces and Melvin is Amy's husband.

Etheleen, Melvin and Amy

Buckskin Bessie

Written on the back: Melvin and Marshall
James Collection

Marshall on Bessie's horse with the famous saddle
that that was a gift from Joe Miller.

One More Parade

Bessie and Marshall
James Collection

Buckskin Bessie

Stevens Collection

Alma continues:

I intended writing about father long ago but just put it off. I think bronchitis was the start of his illness. You know he has had that for years. Dr. said his lungs filled and he had got so weak he didn't have strength to raise anything. He was nothing but skin and bones when he passed away he was so thin. But he was so easy to take care of always satisfied with everything. The boys were sure good to him. Betty was there too but did not offer to help take care of him she said she didn't know how she hated to be around sick people. Grandma was sick too, she has high blood pressure and it goes to her head at times she has funny spells at times. The boys said she was so mean to Grandpa. He had been sick about a month when I went down but not in bed and then I stayed two weeks but he did not suffer he didn't seem to have any pain. Now if you know anything about a will please write and tell about it at once. It would still hold good if it can be found. Do you know if they had a lawyer and who he was. It should be on record. The boys have looked everywhere for it but can't find it. They felt sure that father had it all fixed up he was always so careful with his business. It may be that Grandma done away with it as she told me right away that she knew there was no will. All she was after was fathers money and her children are helping along they had a lawyer hired before the funeral. It must be found before Dec. 9 That is the last day, after that it would not be any good so when you get this letter please write and tell me at once what you know about it.

Jonas Herberg (Bessie's father) died July 13, 1930 in Ruthton, Minnesota. On the death certificate, Art Herberg (his son and Bessie's brother) was the informant and not his second and current wife, Margaret Herberg. Oddly, Art lists his father's wife as Bertha Herberg, Arthur's mother and Jonas' first wife who preceded him in death in 1918.

The estate of Jonas Herberg was not settled until January of 1936, six years after Jonas's death and even four years after his wife Margaret died. The final decree basically says that while Margaret Herberg was alive, she was entitled to his personal property and one-third interest in the real-estate but upon her death, it was then divided equally among his birth children: [4]

Alma Hislop, daughter
Esther Patwell, daughter
Betty Blackwell, daughter
Albert Herberg, son
Peter Herberg, son
Arthur Herberg, son

This is important to note because on Bessie's death certificate (to follow later), Marshall states that Bessie's only survivor was himself, Marshall Blackwell. Yet here in 1936 (seven years prior to her

---

[4] *Minnesota Historical Society Reference Librarian, Brigit Shields*

death), she inherited property from her father along with her brothers and sisters as Betty Blackwell and he is seen above in the picture with her niece's husband, Melvin. Possibly he forgot? According to her nieces, they had been separated for a long period of time prior to Bessie's death, so he may not have known that she received this inheritance or had these stocks. He did not apply for them in his claim on her estate as will be revealed.

Chapter 12

Nothing but Ashes

Buckskin Bessie

Ponca City News, September 6, 1943

Whiteagle Woman Burned in Store

9-6-43

The body of a woman, believed that of Mrs. Marshall Blackwell, about 50, was removed early Monday morning from the Whiteagle store which burned during the electrical storm earlier in the morning, according to Harold Mead, deputy sheriff.

The store, owned by the Blackwells, is located on state highway 40 south of Ponca City at the entrance to the Whiteagle reservation. Blackwell was at Ardmore where he manages a second store. He was expected to return to Ponca City Monday afternoon.

Whether or not the fire was caused by lightning is unknown, police said.

The body of the woman, found near the kitchen cabinet in the living quarters of the store, was badly burned. It was taken to the E. M. Trout & Sons funeral home.

Courtesy of Ponca City librarian... Kimberlee Yeakley

A copy of the record from the Front Funeral Home follows. For the sake of clarity, it is noted that the charges for the burial are to go to Marshall Blackwell in Ardmore, Oklahoma. The order was given by Louis Blackwell, in person. This copy of record was sent from a request to the Ponca City Library and the writing seen on the right is the librarian, L.B.

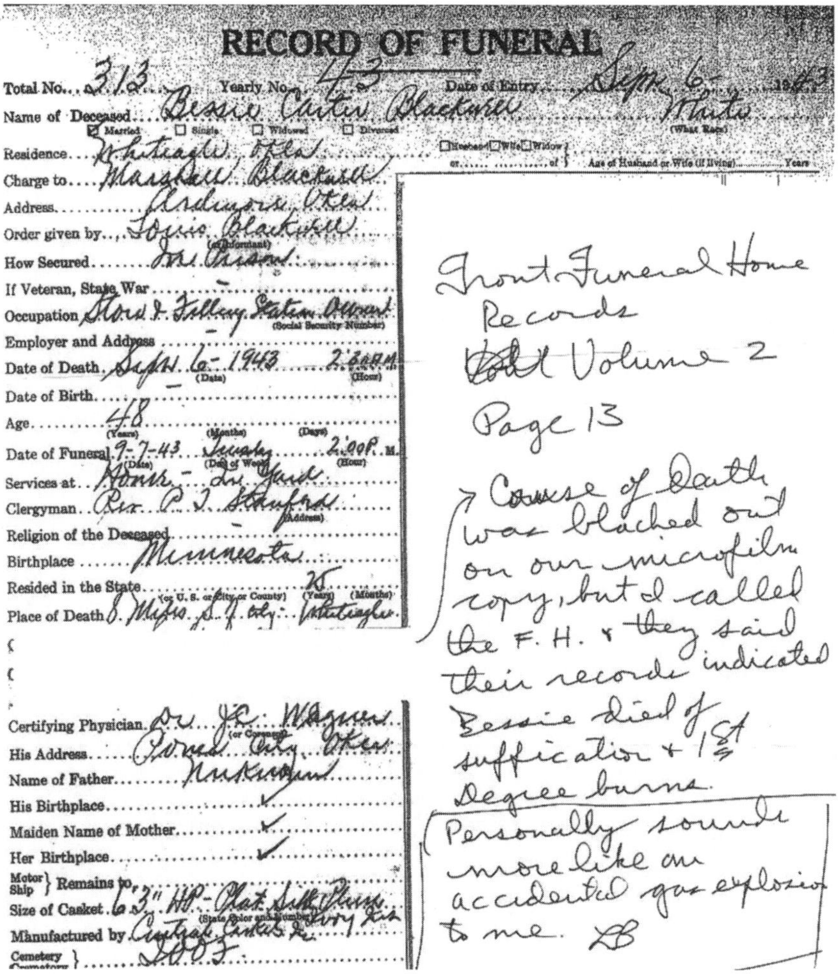

RECORD OF FUNERAL

Total No. 313 Yearly No. 45 Date of Entry Sept. 6, 1943
Name of Deceased Bessie Carter Blackwell White
☑ Married ☐ Single ☐ Widowed ☐ Divorced
Residence Whiteagle, Okla.
Charge to Margaret Blackwell
Address Ardmore, Okla.
Order given by Louis Blackwell
How Secured In Person
If Veteran, State War
Occupation Store & Filling Station Owner
Employer and Address
Date of Death Sept. 6 1943 2:30 A.M.
Date of Birth
Age 48
Date of Funeral 9-7-43 Tuesday 2:00 P.M.
Services at Home - In Yard
Clergyman Rev. P. J. Stanford
Religion of the Deceased
Birthplace Minnesota
Resided in the State
Place of Death I. Miss. J. T. City Whiteagle
Certifying Physician Dr. J. R. Wagner
His Address Ponca City, Okla.
Name of Father Unknown
His Birthplace ✓
Maiden Name of Mother ✓
Her Birthplace ✓
Motor/Ship } Remains to,
Size of Casket 6' 3" HP Flat Silk Plush
Manufactured by Central Casket &
Cemetery/Crematory }

[handwritten margin notes]
Front Funeral Home Records Old Volume 2 Page 13

Cause of Death was blacked out on our microfilm copy, but I called the F.H. & they said their records indicated Bessie died of suffication + 1st Degree burns.

Personally sounds more like an accidental gas explosion to me. SB

Interestingly, the librarian went on to write, "It must not have been questioned very much, otherwise her funeral would have been delayed... she died early morning, of Sept. 6th and the funeral was the 7th. The funeral home records indicate she died of suffocation and 1st degree burns, which would be in the info on her death certificate. I contacted the sheriff's office, they said if you contacted them, they would look into their records, but doubted they would have info since death occurred on Indian land and jurisdiction. The White Eagle

Police might have info but I seriously doubt it."

Louis Blackwell most likely was Marshall Blackwell's brother. Did he live in Ponca City? The only information found on Louis Blackwell was a 1930 U.S. Federal Census that listed him as a son, born in 1887, and living with parents, Dan and Mary Blackwell. There were also two granddaughters living with them at that time that were of mixed blood. They were living in Cherokee, Oklahoma, which is 78 miles west of Ponca City.

A copy of the death certificate for Bessie follows and is easily seen. It records her parents as unknown, her birthplace unknown other than the state of Minnesota, and her birth date unknown. It is signed Marshall Blackwell. How is this possible that he does not know her birthplace or her birth date when they had been married for at least 13 years?

I.O.O.F. Cemetery
Ponca City, Oklahoma

James Collection

Yes, the death certificate states her birth date as unknown but on her tombstone (as you can see from this picture above), it is listed as 1896. Who gave this incorrect date? Her birth date was 1885. Also, note that Marshall has chosen to be buried with her.

In the following news clipping and also in the two newspaper articles above, it stated that Bessie was 48 years old. In truth, she was 58 years old at the time of her death. The information that is used for newspapers is normally gathered from the family, but oddly in all the legal documents, that information was declared unknown.

Buckskin Bessie

Ponca City News, September 7, 1943

Services Are Held For Mrs. Blackwell

Former Cowgirl, She Had Many Souvenirs Of Her Rodeo Days

Friends from all walks of life paid tribute Tuesday afternoon to Mrs. Besse Carter Blackwell, 48, former world's champion cowgirl, who perished early Monday when her home burned.

The services were held beneath a huge tree near the home and under which Mrs. Blackwell often rested. The Rev. P. T. Stanford of Ponca City conducted the services after a noon ceremonial by the Ponca Indians.

Mrs. Blackwell had managed a store at the Whiteagle grounds for many years and had numerous friends among the Ponca Indians. Her home was adjoined directly to the store, and it was this building which was burned during the electrical storm early Monday. Whether or not fire was caused by lightning was unknown, police stated.

Relics Reflect Life

The numerous relics which decorated her home were reflective of the colorful and once fabulous life of Mrs. Blackwell. Associated with the 101 Ranch Wild West show during its hey-day, she included among her keepsakes a picture of Buffalo Bill, autographed by him personally for her, and a priceless diamond and ruby studded saddle, won in 1921 at the Pendleton, Ore., roundup. The saddle has been displayed in Ponca City at a number of Cherokee Strip celebrations.

Her pets included a huge Great Dane, generally seen in the yard of her home, a sorrel saddle horse, plus a number of brilliantly hued peacocks.

Here for 25 Years

Somewhat brusque in her attitude toward people, Besse Blackwell was best liked by those close to her. Born in Minnesota, she had lived in the Ponca City vicinity about 25 years.

Her only survivor is her husband, Marshall Blackwell, who manages a store at Ardmore. He was at Ardmore at the time of Mrs. Blackwell's death.

Burial was in the I.O.O.F. cemetery under the direction of the E. M. Trout & Sons funeral home.

Courtesy of librarian... Kimberlee Yeakley

Nothing but Ashes

Note: Take notice of the information about the Great Dane, as later you will read that a nephew declares this dog was killed right before Bessie died.

In reading the above news clipping, you will see that the Ponca Indians gave Bessie a ceremonial service in addition to that performed by the reverend. Only those who had gained the trust and honor of the Ponca tribe would have been given such a tribute. As was noted earlier, the Indian people included the person's horse in the ceremony and although no longer practiced, in old tribal ways, the horse would have been killed due to the belief that the dead person would then have a mount in the hereafter.[1]

Courtesy of Velma Falconer

Though difficult to see in this picture taken at Bessie's funeral, indeed her sorrel saddle horse is standing among the tribal members. During the Indian ceremony, a peace pipe was to have been presented to the family.[2] Only Marshall Blackwell would have been there to receive it, since he had declared himself her only survivor, and none of her brothers and sisters were informed of her death and able to attend.

[1] *Chronicles of Oklahoma Volume 6, No 3, September, 1928*
[2] *The Real Wild West, pg. 466, Michael Wallis*

Buckskin Bessie

The fire that took Bessie's life occurred in the wee hours of Monday morning, Sept. 6th and in slightly over 36 hours, the authorities notified Marshall Blackwell and his brother, held an investigation, made all the necessary arrangements, and held her funereal services at noon on Sept 7th. None of her family was notified and none were able to attend. The news clipping continues to state that in the fire there was "a priceless diamond and ruby studded saddle that had been displayed at a number of Cherokee Strip celebrations." It does not say, however, that it had been given to her by Joe Miller (as all other records indicate) but rather that she had won it. Oddly, there was not any part of that saddle found in the ruins including the diamonds or silver and gold that would not have burned. Both this article and the earlier one state that Marshall Blackwell was at Ardmore at the time of Mrs. Blackwell's death.

Many different stories have flickered around the mysterious fire and consequent death of Bessie, but the one common thread that runs through them all, *it was neither an act of God nor an accident.*

Below are a few of the different renditions as they were told to me:

"A couple of men took Bessie to a dance that night and after bringing her home they saw the fire as they were a distance away."

"The Indians saw someone leave Bessie's home and then it burst into flames."

"The doors were barred from the outside and the house was set on fire and she could not escape."

"She fell asleep with a cigarette and that is how the fire started."

Later, you will read yet another rendition saying she died in the fire because she would not leave her new fur coat behind.

Nothing but Ashes

LaVerle Stevens (Bessie's niece) has intensely studied her family's genealogy. She kindly shared this interview she conducted with her cousin Dale Herberg on December 28, 2002, shortly before he died:

Our Grandfather, Jonas Herberg, who lived west of Ruthton, Minn. had:
> Over 40 horses
> 100 cattle
> 60 chickens

He was a tailor in the old country. Married a woman who liked to live on a farm. (Britta).

Bessie Herberg had a couple of oil wells given to her by the Millers who had the 101 Wild West Show. She got $125 a month from them during depression days so apparently was not poor. Betty (also called Bessie) had a saddle and bridle with diamond and rubies in them. She met a strange death. It seems that silver dollars along with diamond and rubies disappeared. The gems were all removed from the saddle and bridle, which were also in the fire when her home burned one night. Betty's husband, Marshall Blackwell, claimed the house was struck by lightening. Not true, as it was a perfectly clear night when the fire occurred. Marshall was a close friend of criminal Al Capone, famous back in the 1930s. Neighbors stated there was no lightening that night.

3 brothers at Ruthton, Minn. Albert, Pete and Art. Albert, my Dad, farmed west of Ruthton as did Pete also. Art and wife Laura lived in Ruthton, parents of Dale & Bud. Pete spent $50 on a criminal investigation of Betty's death, which produced nothing. I've been told that Bessie always slept with a gun under her pillow. She also had a dog, apparently for protection. Oddly, somebody either killed or poisoned the dog before her. They tell me she didn't bury the dog during the day but went out at night, dug a hole and buried the dog.

Betty Allen (niece) sent the following newspaper clipping. It appears that this was taken from *The Ruthton Tribune* newspaper, that was in existence in Ruthton, Minnesota, beginning in 1914.

Murder Suspected in Death Former Community Girl

Mr. and Mrs. Art Herberg, who have spent the past two weeks near Ponca City, Oklahoma, where Art's sister, Mrs. Betty Blackwell, was recently found burned to death in her home, returned to Ruthton Sunday evening.

Art says there is a great deal of mystery connected Betty's death as it is thought by many of her neighbors that she came to her death by foul play. Some believe she was murdered and the building set on fire to to cover up the crime.

No trace of the $25,000 saddle she has owned since she rode with the 101 ranch show could be found or any of the valuable diamonds she was known to have possessed. The ruins of the destroyed residence have been searched for some clue that would solve the mystery of her death but without results.

Evidently there are those who are under suspicion in connection with her death but up until this time no arrests have been made and for that matter none may never be made, as on the surface the evidence seems to have been pretty well destroyed.

Courtesy of Pam Hunt

Betty also included a handwritten letter and gave statement to the following:

Marshall Blackwell and Al Capone were good friends and they (Bessie and Marshall) were separated but not divorced and Marshall had a common-law wife and two children by her.

Nothing but Ashes

On September 10th, three days after the funeral services were held; Marshall applied for the estate of Bessie Blackwell. A copy of it follows and he now lists the names of two brothers and one sister (whose name is spelled wrong). In it, he further declares he does not know where they live.

STATE OF OKLAHOMA, KAY COUNTY — ss:

SEP 10 1943

SMILEY, Court Clerk

Bessie Green
DEPUTY

IN COUNTY COURT

To the Honorable __R M Parkhurst_____Judge of the County Court, of the County of Kay, State of Oklahoma:

The Petition of __Marshall Blackwell____of said_____County, respectfully shows:

That__Bessie Blackwell_____, died, intestate, on or about the__5th____ day of __September____, 19_43_, in ____Kay____County of__Kay_____. and State of Oklahoma;

That said deceased, at the time of____her___death, was a resident of_____County of__Kay_____and State of Oklahoma:

That said deceased left estate, real and personal, in said_____Kay_____County, and the value and character of said property, so far as known to your petitioner, are as follows, to-wit:

_____Fire Insurance policy, automobile, horse and about 5 acres _____of land, valued at about $1500.00

That the whole estate and effects for or in respect of which Letters of Administration are hereby applied for, do not probably exceed the value of__Fifteen Hundred_____Dollars;

That the names, ages and residences of the heirs at law of the decedent, so far as known to your petitioner, are as follows:

Marshall Blackwell,	age 48 years, residence	Ardmore, Okla
Arthur Herberg,	age years, residence	unknown
Pete Herberg	age years, residence	unknown
Mrs Hislet	age years, residence	unknown
	age years, residence	
	age years, residence	
	age years, residence	

That due search and inquiry have been made to ascertain if said deceased left any will and testament, but none has been found, and, according to the best knowledge, information and belief of your petitioner, said deceased died intestate;

That your petitioner is_____the husband_____of said deceased, and therefore, as your petitioner is advised and believes, entitled to Letters of Administration of said estate.

Bessie's surviving brothers and sisters also filed claim for her estate with the representation of attorney George W. Miller in Oklahoma (not the brother of Joe) and on March 7, 1944, the State Of Oklahoma, Kay County, made the following ruling concerning the estate of Bessie Carter Blackwell:

ing described estate, to-wit:

CASH: Money from receipt of fire insurance policy and from life insurance policy on said deceased, $4,946.73.

1 Chevrolet Automobile.
1 Horse
65 Shares of stock mentioned in the final account as being Federal Farm Land Bank Stock of Wichita, Kansas.

And the following described real estate:

N½ of N½ of N½ of E½ of E½ of NE¼ of NW¼, Section 34, Township 25, North, Range 2 East,

E½ of E½ of E½ of NE¼ of NW¼, Section 34, Township 25, North, Range 2 East.

S½ of N½ of N½ of the E½ of NE¼ of NW¼, Section 34, Township 25, North, Range 2 East.

South 2 acres off the south side of the E½ of E½ of NE¼ of NW¼, Section 34, Township 25, North, Range 2 East.

Two acres in the S½ of the E½ of E½ of NE¼ of NW¼, Section 34, Township 25, North, Range 2 East.

All of the above described real estate, being in Kay County, State of Oklahoma.

And it further appearing to the Court that the following persons are entitled to distributive shares in said estate in the following proportions, to-wit:

In the shares of stock in the *Ponca City* National Farm Loan Association:

Marshall Blackwell, 1/2 interest
Arthur Herberg, 1/10 interest
Alma Hislop, 1/10 interest
Albert Herberg, 1/10 interest
Peter Herberg, 1/10 interest
Esther Patwell, 1/10 interest

All the rest and residue of said personal property to the surviving husband, Marshall, Blackwell. Said real estate all to the surviving husband, Marshall Blackwell.

Nothing but Ashes

This is only a partial copy of the actual document, but it clearly shows that her brothers and sisters were awarded one-half of the shares of stock that she had. Marshall did not note them in his previous claim, which would indicate that he did not know they existed. It does not tell the value of these shares, but it was valuable enough to be split in half. Were these stocks from the inheritance Bessie received from her father in 1936? Was this money put into shares from the selling of the 50-50 Ranch she and Joe owned together? Or was this simply her life-long savings?

Equally perplexing is the history of this property that Marshall has now inherited that is located at White Eagle. There were a total of five different deeds to this property.

Each deed was sold to Bessie Carter Blackwell from Obie L.S. Buffalo and Ida L.S. Buffalo, his wife, and dated beginning December 1934 through November 1942—transactions that transpired over a nine-year period and ending less than one year before Bessie's death. Marshall Blackwell was not listed as owner on any of these deeds, but after the estate was settled he was awarded the total of four acres by a quit-claim deed on June 23, 1945 (records provided by Sharon Gibson at the Kay County courthouse).

Also perplexing is why is there is only one automobile listed? Would they not have owned at least two cars together? Maybe the answer is that they had already split their personal property between them because of being separated for such a long period of time. If that were true, why didn't they get a divorce? If they were separated, who was paying the premiums on the fire insurance and life insurance policy? Doesn't it seem odd that she would name Marshall as the heir of the property for the fire insurance but didn't name him as having title to it when she bought it only one year prior to her death? It is assumed that being the spouse gives the right to entitlement. We may have to speculate over much of all this, but the one thing that is very clear is Bessie was not a woman without means.

Extra, Extra:

This is a county map of Noble and Kay counties. The property that Bessie and Joe owned together is marked with an X and the dark colored area just above the Kay county line is the property Bessie owned at her death. While they are only about five miles apart, they are worlds apart for Bessie's lifestyle.

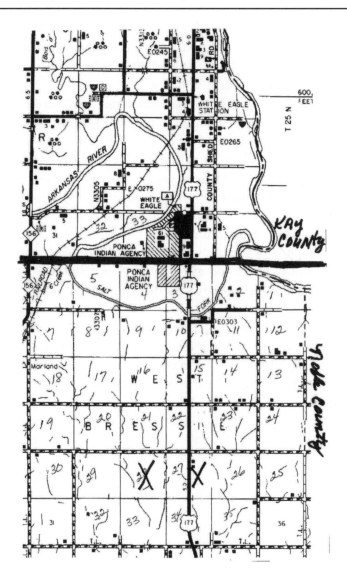

Nothing but Ashes

The two letters that follow were written by Gladys Shane who worked at the Ponca Indian Agency (see map above). They are written to Bessie's niece (Little Bit) Betty Hislop (Fillion) in Hollywood, California in Sept. 1943 in regards to her Aunt Bessie's death. In the first one, we get the other rendition of why she may have perished in the fire.

UNITED STATES
DEPARTMENT OF THE INTERIOR
OFFICE OF INDIAN AFFAIRS
FIELD SERVICE
Pawnee, Okla.
September 17, 1943

Miss Betty Hisslop
Los Angeles, Cal.

Dear Betty:

I should have written you sooner but suppose by now you have heard the sad news about Your Aunt Bessie. Mr. Hron called me the morning of September 6, 1943, and told me her store was burned down. I called later on, after I got to work, and they said they found her body in the NW corner of the back room . I was awfully shocked and felt very badly as I certainly loved Bessie and she loved you lots too and always let me read your letters and always wanted to come to see you. I can hardly yet believe that she isn't there. Everything went with the store. Not one relic or keepsake was saved. Her funeral was under the big tree by the little house in the yard. I am sure that was just as Bessie would have wanted it. She had lots of flowers and lots of her friends were present. Goldie was down in Arkansas when she got word but she came and all the Blackwells were there. I can't help but think Bessie could have gotten out if she had not went after new fur coat. She had just got a new Silver Muskrat and I am sure it was in the cedar chest in the center room. Anway they found pieces of it on her body. I am of the opinion she risked too much and was suffocatedbefore she could leave the building. I am dreadfully sorry about the whole thing and want you to know how badly we all feel and sympathize with you. She did have a full life and I am sure she left in her prime as she was very active and seemed to enjoy her surroundings to the utmost.

Do you still see Nathan Lee? I am sure he must be a very nice chap. He seems to write very nice things home about you. The parents were very happy that he found a friend and they were very well pleased with your picture and after all, Betty, that is all they had to go by . I am sure you are having a good time with all the soldier, sailors, and the marines--to say nothing of the cadets. Keep it up child and have your fun when you can.

Johnnie Hron is to be married soon. The Cuzalina girl is the lucky party. She is very sweet and of course we all loved Johnnie. She wanted a big wedding and is waiting until hehas a furlough.

I will close now and hope to see you sometime. It seems that the binding link between us is perhaps gone but fate may intervene. If I every come to Los Angeles again, I will try to look you up. With kindest regards, I am,

Sincerely,

Gladys Shane

UNITED STATES
DEPARTMENT OF THE INTERIOR
OFFICE OF INDIAN AFFAIRS
FIELD SERVICE

Pawnee, Okla.
Oct. 1, 1943

Dear Betty:

Received your letter a few days ago and should have
written sooner but have been busy and just couldn't find time. I
am sorry that you were not notified sooner of your Aunt Bessie's
passing. Marshall asked me the day of the funeral her address,
the sisters and yours, and I told him J. C. Penny Company was all
I remembered and of course, I could not remember anyone's name but
yours. I also told him to advise Nathan Lee, through his parents,
which must be what happened. I thought Bessie was born in Minnesota
but did not remember where and also thought that the family had nearly
all gone to California to work. Bessie always talked of you and
your mother. But I still don't remember your mother's name nor
the folks in Phoenix that she spoke of often. As I remember, your
brother had a store in Phoenix. Bessie got your letter thanking
her for the jacket and I know she is very happy that you have it.

I would love to have a picture of Bessie and if you have
any films or have any pictures to spare, I would like to have one.
Dr. Klieger and Miss Richardson, the doctor and nurse at the Ponca
Subagency, would also like a photo. We all ate at Bessie's quite
often. She seemed to enjoy having us and occasionally we would furnish
chicken or ham or some other food. It meant that we saved a trip to
town for lunch and I know that Bessie did enjoy having us or she wouldn't
have bothered. Doctor Klieger was in New York on vacation and I wired
him the sad news. He said it ruined his vacation as he was terribly
fond of Bessie and said he was at her store more than at his own home.
I guess you remember that the Doctor's cottage was just about a quarter
of a mile from her place.

It is raining terribly hard here now and I am at the
Otoe Subagency. I have muddy roads home. But I always make it O. K.
in my little Ford which I still have.

Marshall said the store was covered with insurance and
she had life insurance--both made to him. He has someone watching
her place and says he will leave the corner as it is for a while.
He took the horse and will always take care of him, I am sure.

Johnnie Kron got married. I didn't get to see the write
up as I don't take the paper but I guess they had a big wedding.

UNITED STATES
DEPARTMENT OF THE INTERIOR
OFFICE OF INDIAN AFFAIRS
FIELD SERVICE

2.

Bessie was sure counting big on getting to go to Johnnie's wedding and its a shame they weren't married before he went to camp then she could have witnessed it.

I know Bessie would have enjoyed your riding. She was an expert. The Tulsa paper said she was Champion Cow Girl Rider of the World.

Little Bit, I must close. Will look you up if I ever get out there but you know how travel is now so can't make it for a while. If you have the pictures, we would enjoy having them and would be very glad to pay for them.

Love,

Gladys

Betty Hislop (known as Little Bit) in a fur coat that her
Aunt Bessie was to have given her.[3]

[3] *Interview with Maynard Hislop, December 3, 2003*

Buckskin Bessie

A letter from a Pastor's wife

The Woman's Division of Christian Service
of
The Methodist Church

REV. DON J. KLINGENSMITH
SUPERINTENDENT
MRS. DON J. KLINGENSMITH
ASSISTANT SUPERINTENDENT

Ponca Methodist Mission
ROUTE 4
Ponca City, Oklahoma

TELEPHONE 9644-F-11

September 14, 1943.

Miss Bettie Hisslop,
℅ J.C.Penney Co.,
Los Angeles, California.

Dear Bettie,

I am enclosing the card which came with Clifford Roberts flowers for your Aunt Bessie. We wired Clifford as soon as we knew the funeral arrangements, but his flowers though wired, came afterwards. So, Our family took the beautiful orange and yellow wreath and placed it on her grave last Sunday afternoon.

We all do miss her so much and can hardly realize she is gone from our midst. Her funeral was held in her yard among her flowers and by the fish pond which meant so much to her. The pall bearers were all Indian women who were close friends as well as were those who carried and arranged the flowers.

In case you should want to drop Clifford a line, his address is:
Pfc. Clifford Roberts, Dugway Proving Grounds, Tooele, Utah.

Sincerely your friend,

Mrs. Don J Klingensmith

Nothing but Ashes

Enclosed in the letter was the following card from Ponca Floral Company:

With Deepest Sympathy

To some one I will miss

Clifford Roberts

As the author, I have tried not to interject a lot of personal thoughts and feelings throughout this book, but rather have simply given the facts and posed questions to ponder. But this was a difficult place to come to, the end of a life. I want you to know that it's been an exciting adventure discovering all this information. But in that process, however, I also discovered that without any planning on my part, I stood at Bessie's grave on the anniversary of her death. You may say that was just a strange coincidence. I know it was not. But I still wrestled with the question of why? The answer that came was simple. It was a stark reminder that this is not just a story, it was a life—a life that was here and now gone, and it should be honored. It is a befitting tribute to end this chapter with a poem that was written by Joe Miller and found typed on the back of his picture which appears on page 40.

Buckskin Bessie

No Lamentations

I can write no lamentations
On the years that lie behind;
I have treasured up no heartaches
In the background of the mind;
I have left the ghosts of yesterday
For the Life that lies before,
And cremated all the stubble
So it can vex no more.

I waste no time repining
Over tombstones of the past,
For I see the silver lining
Of the clouds that run so fast;
But I never try to stay them,
For more are on the way,
So I close the dark of yesterday
In the sunshine of to-day.

Life is just a moving picture;
And we see it in a glass—
The sorrowful and tragic;
As the figures rise and pass;
So what's the use of weeping?
For before our tears are dry
There comes another picture
With a rainbow in the sky.

J. C. Miller

The Last Picture

James Collection

Buckskin Bessie

Bessie's niece, Betty (Herberg) Allen, acknowledged that this is probably the last known picture of Bessie. She continued to say that her mother took this picture when she and her family visited Bessie in the summer of 1942, one year prior to Bessie's death. The young girl standing next to Bessie is Betty Allen's sister, Merley Herberg. Betty remembers staying in the little cabins near the store and her Aunt Bessie talking about the trip to Alaska that she was planning for later that summer.

As quoted, "she became a crusty old lady, known to give candy to the Indian children."[1]

This perhaps was true but she was always generous,

Thank you, Bessie

[1] *The Real Wild West, pg. 466, Michael Wallis*

Epilogue

Bessie
James Collection

Buckskin Bessie

Below is a letter that I could see Bessie writing to all of us today.

Dear Reader,

It's been quite a ride and I leave you with a few parting thoughts.

It is your right and your privilege to live your life as you choose, but in exchange, you must be willing to accept all the responsibilities and consequences that come from those choices.

Search hard for the positive, the negative is always easy to find. Be flexible, life will have many changes in it and the only way to not break, is to bend.
Don't just walk by, stop to smell those roses!

"Your sins will find you out" was not just a good text, but a real truth. You can depend on it.

I drank exquisite champagne in France and my horse nibbled food from my hand. I enjoyed them both.

As Ever,
Bessie

P.S... Drive a bright yellow car and let them know you are coming.

Bits and Pieces

Remnants of the 101
James Collection

The Old timers Association lends support for the ongoing efforts to restore the historical remains of the 101 Ranch and the restoration of the White Eagle monument that was erected in 1927 in honor of the Ponca chief White Eagle. An application to join this organization can be found at www.kaycounty.info.

The basement of the Marland's Grand Home in Ponca City is filled with items from the 101 Ranch including a scale model of the Wild West show and some wonderful pictures of Buckskin Bessie/Montana Bess.

A special thank you to Darlene Platt.

The Pawnee Bill Museum located in Pawnee, Oklahoma, displayed the Jack Keathly collection of Bessie Herberg, but it may not be there long, as it was for sale.

Extra, Extra:
Save a buffalo head nickel and you will be holding a
piece of the 101 Ranch history;

MILLER BROS & ARLINGTON
101 RANCH
THAT REAL WILD WEST
THE INDIAN CHIEF THAT MADE THE NICKEL FAMOUS
IRON TAIL AMERICA'S REPRESENTATIVE
INDIAN CHIEF
THE 101 BISON THAT CAME FROM 101 RANCH

www.utexas.edu/cola/depts/ams/faculty/Faculty/goetz-
mann/Lectures/Images/CDc/o2020/20-040.jpg

Woolaroc Museum, located in Bartlesville, Oklahoma, displays
a collection of 101 Ranch memorabilia including Joe Miller's exquisite saddle. This fabulous museum also contains a large gun collection, paintings, bronze figures, wildlife, a beautiful lodge, and more.

www.woolaroc.org

There are several private collections of 101 Ranch/Wild West
artifacts. An annual Western Memorabilia Show is held each year in
March in Ponca City where many come to buy, sell, reminisce, and
display their wares.

www.historyoklahoma101.net

Buckskin Bessie

A special thank you to 101 Collector Bob White for sharing his wonderful pictures of Bessie. You are the exception and not the rule!

The amazing restoration of some the pictures found in this book were done by Frank Gary. For more information you can contact him at Neckties Photo Restoration, Legendary Guns (e-mail: frankg47@cox.net).

Beautiful pictures of the 101 Wild West Show performers and their clothing can be found in the book Cowgirls by Flood and Manns, including one on page 60 which lists the lady on the front row as LuLu Parr; clearly yet another case of mistaken identity of Bessie. The picture displays a group of cowgirls from the 101 and Buffalo Bill. Bessie was very proud of her association with Buffalo Bill and displayed an autographed photograph of him in her store.[1] She also had a special pair of gloves given to her by Buffalo Bill with a personal note.[1]

SASS
Single Action Shooting Society

The creation of this sport has grown to include over 70,000 members internationally to date. One of the unique aspects of "Cowboy Shooting" is the requirement to adopt a shooting alias which in turn has created the need for historical research into character and dress (and even a separate competition for accuracy of such portrayal). I am the proud lifetime member as "Buckskin Bessie."

www.sassnet.com/

[1] *The Real Wild West, pg. 465, Michael Wallis*

194

Bits and Pieces

"Memories"
Treasure is the flowing of memories by and by,
resurrected from the past to live again,
in the twinkle of one's eye.

M. J.

The Salt Fork River
James Collection

Buckskin Bessie

Internet research found a distant relative of Bessie's. In this lady's grandmother's trunk of old pictures were some postcards of a woman with a horse and her name was Bessie Herberg. She had no idea who this person was until I contacted her. Perhaps this book will cause you, too, to remember a name of someone or a place that was mentioned, or perhaps you have an old picture that now makes sense. If you would like to add another piece to the puzzle you can @ Buckskinpress.com.

Buckskin Press
7704 W. John Cabot Rd.
Glendale, Arizona 85308
602-547-1942

FOOTNOTES

Introduction
[1] Life in a Wild West Show, pg. 39, Steven Currie

Spreading her wings
[1] The Real Wild West, pg. 307, Michael Wallis
[2] 101 Ranch, pg. xii, Collins and England
[3] 101 Ranch, pg. 164, Collins and England
[4] The Real Wild West, pg. 256, Michael Wallis

101 Wild West
[1] The Real Wild West, pg. 249, Michael Wallis
[2] 101 Ranch, pg. 159, Collins and England
[3] The Real Wild West, pg. 338, Michael Wallis
[4] 101 Ranch, pg. xiv, Collins and England
[5] Ibid, pg. 111
[6] The Real Wild West, pg. 217, Michael Wallis
[7] Life in the Wild West, pg. 25, Stephen Currie
[8] Ibid pg. 28
[9] 101 Ranch, pg. 175, Collins and England
[10] Ibid, pg. 186

On the Road
[1] Life in a Real Wild West Show, pg. 62, Steven Currie
[2] The 101 Ranch, pg. 177, Collins and England
[3] The Real Wild West, pg. 357, Michael Wallis
[4] Edith Tantlinger Diary, University of Oklahoma Library, Western History Collection, Norman, Okla.
[5] The Real Wild West, pg. 357, Michael Wallis
[6] Buffalo Bill and the Enduring West, pg. 79, Hall
[7] The Real Wild West, pg. 429, Michael Wallis
[8] Ibid, pg. 358
[9] The Real Wild West, pg. 428, Michael Wallis
[10] 1911 101 Wild West Roster
[11] 101 Wild West, pg. 467, Michael Wallis
[12] Ibid pg. 360

[13] The Real Wild West, pg. 389, Michael Wallis
[14] Edith Tantlinger Diary, University of Oklahoma Library, Western
    History Collection, Norman, Okla.
[15] The Real Wild West, pg. 391, Michael Wallis
[16] Ibid, Pg. 289

The Trip
[1] The Real Wild West, pg. 398, Michael Wallis

Home is Where The Heart is
[1] The Real Wild West, pg. 400, Michael Wallis
[2] Jack Keathly interview, September 5, 2003
[3] The Real Wild West, pg. 428, Michael Wallis
[4] Authors visit to Wooloroc Museum, March of 2005
[5] Edith Tanlinger Diary, University of Oklahoma Library, Western
    History Collection, Norman, Oklahoma
[6] The Real Wild West, pg. 395, Michael Wallis
[7] Ibid, pg. 424
[8] The Real Wild West, pg. 418, Michael Wallis
[9] Ibid, pg. 429
[10] The 101 Ranch, pg. 30, 34, 35, Collins and England
[11] The Real Wild West, pg. 197, Michael Wallis
[12] Ibid, pg. 459
[13] Ibid, pg. 461

The Scrapbook
[1] The Real Wild West, pg. 278, Michael Wallis

A Place of her Own
[1] The Real Wild West, pg. 466, Michael Wallis
[2] Ponca City (Oklahoma) Courier, March 18, 1915
[3] The 101 Ranch, pg. 233, Collins and England
[4] The Real Wild West, pg. 476, Michael Wallis
[5] Ponca City (Oklahoma Territory) Courier, March 11, 1897
[6] The Real Wild West, pg. 431, Michael Wallis

The Silent Years
[1] The Real Wild West, pg. 466 Michael Wallis
[2] Ibid. pg. 462
[3] The Real Wild West, pg. 500, Michael Wallis
[4] Ibid, pg. 501
[5] Ibid. pg. 504
[6] Ibid. pg. 502
[7] Ibid, pg. 504
[8] Interview with Jack Keathly, Ponca City, Okla. September 5, 2004
[9] The Real Wild West, pg. 515, Michael Wallis
[10] Ibid, pg. 466

One More Parade
[1] The Real Wild West, pg. 466, Michael Wallis
[2] Woolarac collection
[3] The 101 Ranch, back cover, Collins and England
[4] Minnesota Historical Society Reference Librarian, Brigit Shields

Nothing But Ashes
[1] Chronicles of Oklahoma Volume 6, No 3, September, 1928
[2] The Real Wild West, pg. 466, Michael Wallis
[3] Interview with Maynard Hislop, 12/3/03

The Last Picture
[1] The Real Wild West, pg. 466, Michael Wallis

Bits and Pieces
[1] The Real Wild West, pg. 465, Michael Wallis